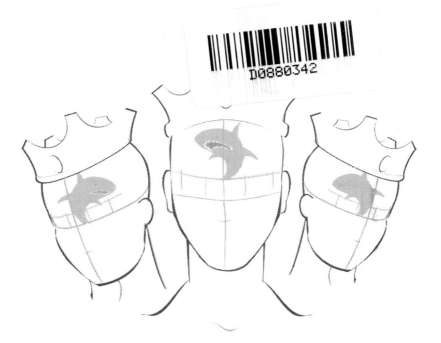

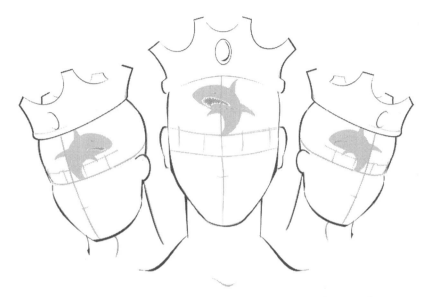

CLUELESS EMPERORS

*How to Overcome Problem People
and Not Be One Yourself*

VICTORIA HUMPHREY

BUZZ

CLUELESS EMPERORS
How to Overcome Problem People and Not Be One Yourself

Victoria Humphrey

PRINT EDITION ISBN: 978-1-939288-16-5
Library of Congress Control Number: 2013939533

www.CluelessEmperors.com

Clueless Emperors® is a registered trademark.

Published by BUZZ,
An Imprint of Wyatt-MacKenzie

NEW DICTIONARY ENTRY

Clueless Emperors [klʊo' lis em'pcr crs] n. [derived from Hans Christian Andersen's story *The Emperor's New Clothes*] 1. People who use power foolishly or selfishly 2. People who halt progress 3. People who suck the life out of you

CONTENTS

Punctuation
Length of a Written Message
The Visible Bottom Line

For Foster

Your intelligence, high energy, and unconditional love amaze me every day.

Introduction

"The only end of writing is to enable the readers better to enjoy life, or better to endure it."
—Samuel Johnson

We don't always get along with each other for a wide variety of reasons. It would be an exceptional person who is logical, kind-hearted, and socially skilled—all the time. Unfortunately, selfish motivation is common and when people behave this way, resolving differences with them isn't easy. Tempers can flare at a moment's notice—even our best intentions can't be counted on to prevent bruised relationships—resulting in stalled progress and communication breakdowns. So we get stressed out, ask our friends for advice, don't get enough sleep, and wonder how to make things better. Without the right skills, our efforts to protect personal "territory" fail, and the final outcome is all too predictable. In the life-isn't-fair department, the person with the highest rank usually prevails, regardless of the facts.

Have you ever clashed with someone whose primary motive seems to be self-promotion at all costs? Disagreeing with a need-to-win person isn't pleasant and hoping for fair and equitable treatment is wishful thinking. To complicate matters, persuading the antagonist to listen to your point of view feels like an impossible assignment. When such a person is taking undue advantage and also has the power to control how things work out for you, who gets the last word?

Any satisfaction we might gain from informing people of their bad behavior—even under our breath—is short-term. Although name-calling may have some blow-off-steam appeal, it also implies a sense of helplessness if labeling their misconduct is all we do. Quietly giving up and giving in when people have the power to shut us down doesn't work either—it just makes their job easier, and our lives more stressful.

Understanding the root cause of power struggles can significantly improve the odds of being successful. To help with that, the term "Clueless Emperor" provides insight into their self-centered ways:

- They're clueless about any form of common good.
- They add a misuse of control or authority to the mix.
- They act like emperors in whatever setting—and toward whatever people—they're able to dominate.

Looking at problem behavior through this lens provides clues for recognizing the force that drives inappropriate actions. People in a Clueless-Emperor state of mind, regardless of the territory they control, have one trait in common: *they use their power foolishly or selfishly.* And they certainly do suck the life out of people who lack the skills to stand up for themselves. Clueless Emperor behavior is pervasive. We may work with people who behave this way, or socialize with them, do business with them, and even live with them. And sometimes we are them.

Clueless Emperors—especially when there is no opposition—cause hardship with wide-ranging penalties: from benign to life altering. In extreme cases, people die as a result of their destructive actions. When circumstances give them the power to ensure an outcome—guaranteed to be in *their* best interests—problems are inescapable. Some skilled individuals have the talent to prevail when Clueless Emperors obstruct progress, but most people are immobilized, like deer in headlights. They're also clueless, but in a very different way, and for a very different reason: *they have less power than the Clueless Emperors taking advantage of them and don't know how to take care of their own needs.*

Abusing authority for personal gain is a historical equalizer, so Clueless Emperors' misconduct is certainly nothing new. It's also not new that people in the vicinity of Clueless Emperors often feel the pressure to conform. So why does this kind of exploitation persist? The answer lies in understanding certain characteristics of human nature that influence behavior and motivation. Once armed with appropriate knowledge, the next step is developing the skills to prevail—the mechanics of which are described in these pages. The tactics and strategies provided here will help readers achieve Clued-In status, which affords several advantages. These benefits are the value proposition offered in this book:

- advancing career objectives
- achieving goals while serving the common good
- building trusting relationships
- managing conflict successfully
- leading a low-stress life

Although my primary goal is to help people overcome the Clueless Emperors in their future, readers will also learn to heed personal warning signals in order to avoid irresponsible behavior of their own making. Clued-In citizens know that it's important to recognize and manage any personal tendencies along these lines.

My education and career in sales, organizational development, and human resources have taught me how to overcome Clueless Emperors, despite their power and authority. Although it was never my original intent, the profession I chose made it imperative for me to gain this knowledge. With decades of experience behind me, I wrote this book to share what I've learned so you can achieve the same skill with more speed, and less pain, than if trial and error were your only teachers. Fuzzy platitudes have been kept to a minimum here, but specific and actionable guidance is plentiful. There is a way to overcome Clueless Emperors and not be one yourself—and I'm going to show you how to do it.

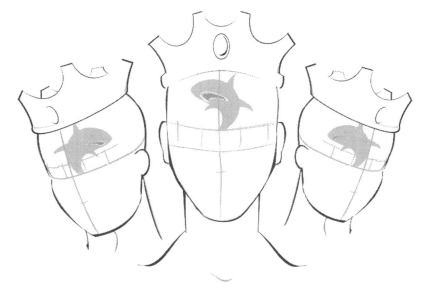

PART 1
The Basics

Clueless Emperors 101

"Nothing is more terrible than ignorance in action."
—Johann Wolfgang von Goethe

If people misusing power and taking advantage of well-meaning citizens has ever been a problem for you, this book has information and guidance to help overcome these challenges. When selfish opportunists are on the loose, having effective skills is crucial. Although it's reasonable to expect fair treatment, and the freedom to thrive in a world without unwarranted interference, life doesn't always turn out that way. When reasonable people lack the know-how to hold their ground, they can't effectively stand up for themselves in conflict situations. Although that goal may seem unattainable, there is a solution for those who want to succeed: the skills required to overcome Clueless Emperors are easily within your grasp—really. This chapter starts your exciting journey from the war-torn land of the uninformed to the tropical paradise of the Clued-In.

Although the term "emperor" is used throughout the book, it's certainly not meant to imply that empresses are off the hook! Clueless Emperors come in different sizes, shapes, colors, ages, and genders. Unfortunately they can't be recognized on sight—bad behavior is their calling card—so the ability to quickly assess when they're in the vicinity provides advantages.

Clueless Emperors remind me of a human version of sharks: we don't always know where they are, so it's important to be on the lookout—their strikes can be sudden and painful. We know that sometimes they bite and sometimes they don't—their behavior is unpredictable. We know that when they do bite, it can be very serious, sometimes people die, so we need to protect ourselves against them. Just as with sharks, if the victims of Clueless Emperors don't know how to ward off threatening behavior, they're forced to live with the damage left behind. Although the art of communication is always valuable, it becomes an extraordinary asset when Clueless Emperors are causing problems. Here are ways to identify them:

- They always make certain their own needs get met, no matter who or what gets sacrificed in the process.
- They do their best to ensure less powerful challengers are quickly put out of action, no matter how worthwhile the objectives of those challengers may be.
- They love to show off and want everyone to know how important they are while committing a wide assortment of behavioral transgressions.

Clueless Emperors masterfully control their environment by using power foolishly or selfishly to push their own agendas—with no regard for the common good. They don't feel like they've won, unless those who have disagreed with them have lost. They don't seek opportunities for mutual gain, because that concept has never occurred to them. They don't think about talented people or good ideas that get crushed. They get what they want, when they want it. If you are in their way, it's important to learn how to maintain composure and think rationally, or be prepared for defeat.

Even though logic dictates that acknowledging problems

is the first step toward fixing them, don't count on Clueless Emperors choosing this path—they take care of their own needs without consideration of a broader point of view. Facts are irrelevant, and logic doesn't apply. No doubt, problem-solving skills are required to get around Clueless Emperors, but intellect and logic alone are often not enough to compensate for their sheer power. This book helps you with a unique set of skills that compensates for a lack of power on your part: *behavioral skills* are a key ingredient to overcoming Clueless Emperors.

Lots of very smart people don't have a clue about effective behavioral skills—what they are, or how to develop them. You will get detailed instructions here that include tips for how to be effective with a wide variety of people in your life—from family members and friends—to work colleagues at all hierarchical levels, bosses included.

A fairy tale I loved as a child, "The Emperor's New Clothes," inspired me to think of foolish, selfish people as Clueless Emperors. The story was written by Hans Christian Andersen way back in 1847, so this kind of behavior is obviously not a recent event! For those who missed this fairy tale, or perhaps no longer recall the details, a retelling can be found in Appendix A. In short, the main character is a know-it-all emperor who behaves selfishly, and doesn't have a clue about his own foolishness.

Over quite a long period of time, those in the emperor's inner circle act as if they don't notice his self-centered ways and collectively keep up a charade to protect themselves from the fallout of speaking openly to their employer. Not surprisingly, the local residents follow their example and adopt the same behavior for fear of losing their livelihoods. The degree to which the townspeople turn a blind eye to their predicament might seem irrational, but their reality makes them afraid to speak up—so they pretend their environment is a happy place to live and work.

Finally and thankfully, justice prevails at the story's conclusion, and the emperor gets what he deserves. The catalyst that brings the facts to light comes from a surprising source—it's a child's innocent remark that breaks the empire's communication logjam. But then, that's why we call the story a fairy tale. Several life lessons from Andersen's educational narrative are explored and analyzed here, specifically two important messages for grown-up readers:

1. Take action when someone's abuse of power negatively affects you.
2. Use your own power responsibly.

Perhaps if this book had been available in the mid-nineteenth century, the emperor might have avoided the humiliation he ultimately suffered. But then, perhaps not, because Clueless Emperors are rarely interested in self-improvement—in their minds, they are nothing short of perfect, and we should never count on them to do the right thing.

Even though Andersen's fairy tale seems uncomplicated on the surface, it reveals a complex aspect of human nature at its core: he ever so gently reminds us that people with power are capable of abusing it while creating all manner of misery for others. He also lets us know that we have choices when managing power—other people's as well as our own. The central characters in the story would have experienced a more agreeable outcome had they been Clued-In to the skills that would have prevented their problems in the first place, including the emperor himself.

Over the years, the fairy tale has become a metaphor for the social custom of people not speaking candidly—especially to those who misuse power—even when the truth is nakedly apparent. This aspect of human nature poses some interesting questions:

- Why can't we count on people to consistently acknowledge the truth once they become aware of it?
- What can we do when faced head-on with people who do not, or will not, acknowledge obvious reality?
- Why did the emperor perpetuate the sham even *after* he realized that the longer he continued to pretend, the more foolish he seemed?

I will try to answer these questions and explain the motivation behind Clueless Emperors' misconduct, and the reason they carry on with plans they know are wrong. Hoping for an innocent child to show up and save the day isn't a practical strategy. It may work in children's stories, but it certainly doesn't work that way in real life.

Understanding the skills and achieving the skills, however, are two very different things, so this book ensures you have the expertise for both. With the right skills in hand, there isn't a need to feel helpless when Clueless Emperors interfere and take advantage of their power. Everyone can benefit from the advice in these pages, because Clueless Emperor predicaments are so common. The tips offered here are especially valuable, because they're not easily accessible:

- Most of us don't have communication-savvy family members, advisers, or mentors to teach us the skills.
- Our educational system doesn't teach them.

Although some of the material in this book can be found in other resources, you won't find it integrated under one cover as it is here. The skills are easy to understand as individual behaviors, and when practiced in combination, they become the formula that discourages Clueless Emperors. You'll find many examples that illustrate the recommendations, and each chapter's conclusion has a "Main Points" summary for easy review of the material. By following the advice and suggested exercises, readers will be able to develop the ability to achieve goals despite attempts to stifle their progress.

When valuable thoughts and ideas are squashed, Clueless Emperors don't care because they are, well, *clueless*. To add insult to injury, by definition, their actions are dead wrong. When people are Clued-In and use their power wisely, they should be respected and followed. It's the *combination* of power and cluelessness that's destructive. *This point needs to be emphasized.* History has shown that power tends to corrupt, but we shouldn't assume this is always the case—there are noteworthy exceptions. It's important to objectively evaluate problems based on their own unique characteristics, and the information coming up will help you do just that.

The expertise gained here can also be applied to short-term or infrequent encounters with Clueless Emperors who are exasperating at a particular moment in time. For example, think about customer service representatives who are not Clued-In about their role to serve customers and prove that lack of knowledge by disregarding the very people they're being paid to help. Standing in long lines or waiting on hold (*the "your-call-is-very-important-to-us" recording that plays over and over isn't convincing*) only to be "rescued" by a clueless customer service person is not my idea of a good time. Regrettably, it's often the only choice when we're in their clutches.

The customer service function in many companies needs a major overhaul. Countless business articles over the years confirm this sad reality. The companies themselves can't seem to fix the problem, so perhaps frustrated customers can lend a hand by making use of the information in this book to encourage better service: savvy, Clued-In customers with effective skills have a better chance of getting their needs met than customers who don't have a clue about how to get the service they deserve.

Gaining awareness of Clueless Emperors' motives improves the odds of overcoming them. Specifically, recognizing why Clueless Emperors win so often will equip readers to find effective ways to disagree with them, even in the face of their power. Sometimes Clueless Emperors behave irresponsibly out of sheer habit and don't comprehend why the people around them feel stressed out. In other cases, they *do* know— and just don't care. Whether they know better or not, challengers who lack the skills to overcome them become pawns. Or worse.

A good starting point for a Clueless Emperor 101 education is to watch any news broadcast or scan any newspaper and take notice of people who love the limelight. As an example, politicians often provide excellent public illustrations of people who abuse power and behave ridiculously. Just look for stories about people who use their power in foolish or selfish ways— a Clueless Emperor will be right there. Even though the stories that make headline news featuring high-profile Clueless Emperors grab our interest, the low-profile ones aren't much different—they're just not well-known. Clamoring for attention is their favorite sport, and not getting caught breaking rules is the goal.

Many businesses, corporations, and governments of all sizes work hard to keep their local Clueless Emperor debacles hush-hush. Even though many of them make every effort to conceal wrongdoing (the tobacco industry comes to mind), their shenanigans—or many times worse—have made big news in the past few years. A spotlight was directed at this problem in an article in *Crain's New York Business* (July 23, 2012), featuring a boutique firm that specializes in controlling public relations nightmares for their clients. The article says that hiring these types of firms for damage control is becoming more and more common, but warns their services don't come cheap. The story goes on to reference a survey done by Spencer Stuart and Weber Shandwick: 71% of large companies have experienced a reputation-threatening crisis within the past two years. *Wow—that number certainly corresponds to a lot of bad behavior!*

Although the article focuses on the public relations firms themselves (high-profile clients like Bernie Madoff and Dominique Strauss-Kahn are cited), one has to wonder why so much bad behavior was tolerated in the first place—to the point that high-priced damage control was required to suppress it. It's not hard to imagine that people using power foolishly or selfishly are somehow involved. It's safe to say that keeping Clueless Emperors around can be expensive.

Although disagreeing with Clueless Emperors is never fun, achieving independence from them is important, because they can show up anywhere at any time. Unless you're a hermit, there isn't an option to be out of harm's way. Left unchecked, it's common for Clueless Emperors to gang up with disastrous results:

- Families with multiples of them are dysfunctional.
- Organizations led by them go out of business or need bailout money from taxpayers to survive.
- Countries governed by them experience political upheaval, economic havoc, terror and violence.

Nearly everyone has been squeezed by a Clueless Emperor or two—or maybe more?—and because it's so unpleasant to be in their grip, you may have chosen to go along with them out of self-protection. My goal is to help you discourage people with self-serving intentions for a Clueless-Emperor-Free future. That said, overcoming an Emperor may not occur with every attempt, so I also address what to do with challenging situations that can't be resolved satisfactorily. There are circumstances when a departure strategy is the most sensible choice, but you'll want the certainty of having done your best before exiting the scene of the crime.

There is no reason to give up or give in any longer. The counsel here doesn't offer bulletproof protection, but it does provide a Kevlar-like vest. Beyond protection, there are also some effective strategies that will facilitate getting your needs met easily and smoothly, without acrimony, no matter how many obstacles are thrown your way.

Chapter 1 Main Points
Clueless Emperors 101

- Clueless Emperors are everywhere.
- Clueless Emperors and their victims have cluelessness in common; power is the differentiator between them.
- Clueless Emperors blatantly misuse their authority and impose penalties on anyone who doesn't fall in line, so conflicts are inevitable.
- It's possible to learn skills and get Clued-In, so overcoming Clueless Emperors becomes a reality.
- Any motivated person can learn the skills.

> *"I had no idea there was a special name for people who behave like I used to."*
> —A Recovering Clueless Emperor

The Clueless Emperor Profile

*"It is not because things are difficult that we do not dare; it is
because we do not dare that they are difficult."*
—Seneca

Clueless Emperors have a personality profile that's one
of a kind. To overcome them, it's helpful to understand everything possible about their characteristics and motives. We'll
start this chapter with some frequently asked questions to give
you a sense of how they operate:

**1. Why are sharks illustrated on the cover of this book? Do
they have something in common with Clueless Emperors?**

*Certainly, both are predators. But their similarities go beyond
this obvious commonality. New research in the last decade indicates sharks are not the mindless, ruthless man-eaters we thought
them to be. They are sociable and curious, but like Clueless
Emperors, they have selfish motives and can't be trusted. This is
what makes both sharks and Emperors so dangerous. They draw
us in (literally and figuratively), and then decide whether to bite
us. When it comes to real sharks, we have a choice to stay out of
the water. With Clueless Emperors, there is no choice. If we want
to live in the real world, they are a force to be reckoned with and
a challenge to overcome. The cover of this book depicts Clueless
Emperors with sharks for brains as a reminder of their capability
to harm.*

2. How often do Clueless Emperors show up?

It's the frequency of our interactions with people (family members, friends, professional colleagues, or service providers are examples) that dictates the number of Clueless Emperor encounters we'll have. But it's hard to predict exactly where or when this will happen, so it's essential to be observant and have the skills to act at a moment's notice.

It's not uncommon for some people to experience multiple occurrences weekly. In difficult work or family situations, Clueless Emperor encounters can occur several times a day. In these extreme cases, prospects for satisfactory results seem unattainable and stress levels can become unbearable.

3. When is it important to be on the lookout for a Clueless Emperor who could pose a problem?

Clueless Emperors are probably lurking when you don't feel free to express yourself. There is pressure to keep your head down and stay under the radar. You might feel a desire to escape. All these feelings will pass when you discover there are skills available to address these situations head-on and be successful.

4. What motivates Clueless Emperors to behave badly?

Sometimes Clueless Emperors use their power to block progress for no other reason than because they can. They like calling attention to their importance, because they're full of themselves and love to show off. Sometimes they simply don't know any better, or don't realize what they're doing. But most often, they consciously and selfishly advance their agendas for personal gain, and treat other people's needs as trivial or of no consequence. They have no sense of civility when they want something and can't get it quickly. Instant gratification is their lifeblood.

Clueless Emperors use their power to discount people's input, abilities, and feelings without regard to any ideas or solutions those individuals might have contributed had they been free to have a say. If this is happening to you, pay attention. Ignoring conflict doesn't make problems go away. People eventually suffer when they deny anything untoward is taking place, even when it's right in front of their eyes.

5. What are the signs a Clueless Emperor is nearby?

Before answering this question specifically, it's important to remember that sometimes bad outcomes occur when there isn't a Clueless Emperor in sight. Knowledge or information required for a good decision is simply missing or ignored out of innocence, not malfeasance. People are giving their best effort to solve a problem, but they don't know what they don't know.

A Clueless Emperor is nearby when misconduct comes into play. Facts are withheld or crushed through a foolish or selfish misuse of power. How will you know the difference? Clueless Emperors are experts at ignoring people who would contribute if given a chance. An example might be when flaring tempers prevent information flow. Using inappropriate words or tones of voice that intimidate others to the point they stop talking is a common misuse of power.

Conversely, when Clueless Emperors themselves have pertinent information that isn't compatible with their selfish goals, they keep it to themselves for self-centered reasons. Although this circumstance can be harder to detect, a key indicator is lack of information-sharing. The Enron Corporation scandal and the company's subsequent downfall is a good example of executives who withheld information and privately colluded to misrepresent the company's financial data. They committed this crime to drive up the corporation's stock price for the sole purpose of increasing their personal wealth with no regard for employees or share-

holders. (From the CNBC documentary *The Smartest Guys in the Room,* 2005.)

6. How do Clueless Emperors respond when a challenger is successful?

Sometimes they learn from the experience and become more civilized as a result. More often, however, they don't learn a thing and remain clueless. Do not feel sorry for them when this occurs. This book is designed to help you overcome Clueless Emperors, not cure them. They are responsible for their own development. If the Clueless Emperors you overcome happen to have an "aha!" learning moment along the way, that's great. But transforming personalities and reforming character flaws should not be your primary mission. Some of these scoundrels are very tough and resist change at all costs.

The goal is to neutralize power and get all perspectives taken into account, not necessarily repair an Emperor's inability to collaborate. Having said that, this book is designed to teach skills that may cause Clueless Emperors to discover the error of their ways and behave less imperiously. It's a great side benefit when this happens.

7. What is the likelihood of overcoming a Clueless Emperor?

Clueless Emperors come with different levels of power and nastiness. The more treacherous they are, the more difficult it is for any individual person to overcome them. This book teaches skills that provide the communication know-how and negotiation ability to succeed in most circumstances, but you need to calculate the risk before taking on this challenge. Most Clueless Emperors are manageable, but some of them are quite dangerous. This book helps with that, too, and offers realistic alternatives if you run into one whose ability to harm goes beyond your scope.

8. Do Clueless Emperors behave badly all the time?

A quotation by Abraham Lincoln sheds light on this question. Although his words are about gullibility, they can be reinterpreted to exemplify the Clueless Emperor dynamic. Lincoln provided insight about how often people are fooled when he said:

> **"It is true that you may fool all the people some of the time;**
>
> **you can even fool some of the people all the time;**
>
> **but you can't fool all of the people all of the time."**

When we understand what Lincoln was suggesting, we're able to infer how frequently people behave like Clueless Emperors:

- *No one is a Clueless Emperor all the time. (Whew!)*

- *Some people are Clueless Emperors a lot of the time. (Unfortunately.)*

- *All of us are Clueless Emperors some of the time. (Yes, it's true.)*

Although they can be tricky and mean-spirited, Clueless Emperors don't usually behave that way full-time. Some people are exceptions to this general principle, but they are in the minority. The term "Clueless Emperor," as it's used in this book, is an abbreviated way of saying "when someone acts like a Clueless Emperor at a particular moment in time."

Even though unrelenting Clueless Emperor behavior isn't common, some people do behave this way with regularity and cause problems wherever they go—their self-absorbed condition keeps them isolated from reality. If you're the target of a Clueless Emperor like this, don't ever count on civilized conduct—their bad behavior should never come as a surprise.

Sometimes people do surprise us, however, when they act like Clueless Emperors only occasionally—after all, predicting how any one person might use his or her power in any given situation is not a precise science. Indeed, it's what makes human beings so complex. When people behave badly, it's easy to forget their positive attributes—and when they behave with civility, it's easy to forget their potential for ruthlessness. Thoughtful consideration and heartless self-indulgence in the same person are not mutually exclusive.

One of America's most controversial presidents, Lyndon Johnson, illustrates this dynamic very well. Robert Caro's four biographies of the 36th U.S. President vividly capture how Johnson dramatically and consistently exercised his power for both good and ill purposes, revealing how difficult it can be to predict human behavior.

Last but not least, we must attend to our inner Clueless Emperor, because everyone has occasion to misuse power from time to time. When we're conscious of this potential within ourselves, less effort is required to avoid misconduct. If you're wondering how your own behavior fits into this model, Chapter 5 provides clues.

9. Would there ever be a reason to deliberately avoid Clueless Emperors?

The short answer is "yes," but there is more to consider. Let's assume for a moment that you read this book from cover to cover, understand the skills taught in the final chapters, practice the skills, and master them. Your newfound expertise has given purpose to your life: you feel a calling to eradicate Clueless Emperors from the planet.

STOP!!

If a Clueless Emperor's behavior does not have negative

implications for you personally, or for people with whom you're aligned, it's advisable to walk away. When you have no vested interest in the outcome of a particular conflict, choosing to insert yourself in someone else's disagreement is generally unwise and unnecessarily risky. In other words, do not set yourself up as a one-person Clueless Emperor S.W.A.T. team. Your time is better spent closer to home, overcoming Clueless Emperors who affect your own life.

If you feel compelled to help the victim of a Clueless Emperor, even though the circumstances have nothing to do with you personally, make sure the victim is open to advice before proceeding. Some people prefer to whine and complain without accepting responsibility for their inaction. They take pleasure wallowing in misery and enjoy feeling sorry for themselves. They may even resent an intrusion on their pity party. It is their right, after all, to behave childishly. In these circumstances, the most sensible action is to leave these crybabies alone.

The answers to these frequently asked questions are intended to provide a glimpse into the Clueless Emperor personality, and why their decision-making causes so much failure. Think about some bad decisions that have negatively affected you: it's likely they can be traced to a misuse of power. This is what the majority of failures have in common, which is why the physical skills taught in the final chapters of this book contribute to effective decisions and fewer conflicts.

It doesn't help to know that when Clueless Emperors selfishly wield their muscle for personal gain, their misdeeds often catch up with them. Regrettably, karma can sometimes take a while to arrive. In the meantime, life for the Clueless Emperors' victims is painful. If you choose to tackle an Emperor head-on without the right skills, it would be less painful to go swimming with sharks instead and end your misery faster. On the other hand, if you've been in cahoots with them, it's time to learn how to defend yourself. People who do nothing to confront Emperors are part of the problem. So why do people collude? Here are two primary explanations:

- They lack courage or self-confidence.
- They fear repercussion if their attempt fails.

Most unskilled people are rightfully concerned about the possible harmful consequences of a confrontation, so they play it safe and take no action—a lack of knowledge and experience makes it difficult to imagine other choices. When would-be challengers can't acknowledge a lack of skill, they invent excuses for their failure to act: they might say they just wanted to be polite, or didn't want to rock the boat. After all, fragile egos must be soothed. But these rationalizations don't help anyone. They merely make it easier for Clueless Emperors to rule.

Make no mistake. Clueless Emperors want the people around them to be submissive. When people don't comply and can't effectively negotiate—they lose. Unfortunately, as people gain effective confrontational skills, they appear more frequently on Clueless Emperors' radar screens. Anyone who gains power and uses it judiciously makes an especially appealing target, because trouncing someone who uses power sensibly makes Clueless Emperors feel extra superior. Fully prepared is safer than partially prepared.

When conflict with a Clueless Emperor threatens to harm you or people with whom you're aligned, it's essential to address the issue and reach a satisfactory resolution. Expertise is imperative in these situations, because skills drive strength. Although it can be challenging to get Clueless Emperors to listen, everyone's ideas should be given consideration, including yours. Here's why: what if a brilliant idea wasn't taken seriously because the person who had it didn't communicate well, allowing a Clueless Emperor to kill it? There are lots of examples in these pages where this very thing has happened. It doesn't make sense for anyone to be dismissed before his or her ideas are even considered, let alone accepted.

Before challenging a Clueless Emperor, it's important to know how many groveling hangers-on are sucking up to that person. Clueless Emperors seldom operate alone. The most influential ones like to surround themselves with sycophants who turn kowtowing into an art form. I call them Clueless Emperor Apprentices, and the more of them there are, the more hazardous the environment they control.

When their power remains unrestricted, Clueless Emperors and associated Apprentices become deeply embedded in the families or organizations they dominate. Sometimes people in their sphere of influence begin to imitate them out of fear. That's why it's crucial to assess how many Apprentices are supporting any particular Clueless Emperor blocking your progress—*before* deciding on a strategy. Never assume they're operating alone.

Left unchecked, Clueless Emperors will proliferate over time and eventually destroy any environment they control. Adolf Hitler's source of power is an extreme example of this dynamic. We must remember, like many other oppressors, he didn't act alone. It wasn't possible to carry out his plan without complicity, so he recruited like-minded people and put them in positions of power. His inner circle used intimidation and fear tactics to push an agenda that unimaginably succeeded for a long period of time.

Even though the horror of Hitler's regime is unparalleled, the model he put into operation isn't unique. It exists in families, private and public companies, and governments. A powerful select few behave badly—sometimes breaking the law—hide what they do and get away with it for a period of time, sometimes long periods of time. Meanwhile, their victims suffer.

Clusters of executive-level Clueless Emperors hanging out together in corporate and government organizations cause no end of problems. For example, in 2008, when our country faced a major financial crisis, it would have been less disastrous if more Clueless Emperor Busters had been around. Many, many thanks to those who refused to collude with the power-mongers, not the least of whom was Brooksley Born, former chair of the Commodity Futures Trading Commission (CFTC). During her tenure from August 1996 to June 1999, Ms. Born repeatedly warned Congress of the need to regulate over-the-counter derivatives and other specific financial instruments, but her concerns were ignored. The lack of regulation in this market contributed to the economic crisis that took hold of the United States several years later—a good example of karma taking a while to arrive.

Although Ms. Born persistently tried to make this point, there were too many Congressional Clueless Emperors blocking her recommendations and drowning out her voice. Had there been a few more Clueless Emperor Busters to support her, the economic disaster that followed may well have been averted. Brooksley Born's efforts were finally, if belatedly, acknowledged when she was chosen as a recipient of the 2009 John F. Kennedy Profile in Courage Award.

The companies that propelled our country into economic failure had plenty of Clueless Emperors on their payrolls. Sadly, taxpayer money would not have been needed to bail them out had there been sufficient numbers of Clueless Emperor Busters working inside those companies, or the government agencies theoretically regulating them. We will never know what might have been, but the odds are, opportunities were missed.

It's tough to go against powerful leaders who control

people's livelihoods, but bystanders who are aware of wrong-doing can make a difference if they're skilled and band together. The lesson here? Never let a lack of skill prevent you from stopping Clueless Emperors who use their power in harmful ways. When Clueless Emperors are doing bad things, the good people who watch and do nothing are helping them. People who learn and apply the skills that prevent Clueless Emperors from succeeding are role models, and they often inspire bystanders to join in and contribute. Develop the right skills, and you can be one of these people.

I hope everyone reading this book will aspire to become a Clueless Emperor Buster in whatever world you inhabit and sphere of influence you enjoy. Keep in mind there isn't a lot of difference between the everyday problems of average citizens and the powerful few. It's just that when the powerful few need to solve their problems, they do it in a way that causes heads to roll. There really is strength in numbers, so just imagine what could happen if a critical mass of people developed the competence to overcome Clueless Emperors who needed to be controlled. Look at it this way:

- One person without power or behavioral skills who confronts a Clueless Emperor is taking a huge risk.
- A group of people without power or behavioral skills who band together to confront a Clueless Emperor are improving their chances, but there is still significant risk.
- One person without power, but *with* behavioral skills, who confronts a Clueless Emperor has a decent chance of succeeding.
- A group of people without power, but *with* behavioral skills, who *band together* to confront a Clueless Emperor have an excellent chance of succeeding. This winning combination is the ultimate resource for long-term

sustainability of any family, organization, or government.

Yes, it can be challenging and even risky to speak up. It's why people often remain silent, even when it means sacrificing their own needs, but there is a safe way to stop colluding. Most people know, whether consciously or subconsciously, that special skills are required to disagree with powerful people. When those without power don't have these skills or can't envision the skills can be learned, they feel safer keeping their thoughts to themselves. Those who try and fail to negotiate with Clueless Emperors seldom feel motivated to persevere. The losses are too painful. They quit and punish themselves instead, but it doesn't make sense to give up—anyone who is motivated can learn the skills.

Each person reading this book has a unique baseline of competencies: those with a sophisticated ability will use the information to add a few new skills or polish what they already know, but readers starting from scratch should have no fear. The required expertise can't be delivered in pill form, but specific recommendations that have the potential to transform lives are in these pages. My promise is that you will not wonder what to do, or where to begin, as you close the back cover. Our contract is simple. I provide the blueprint and building materials, and you provide the desire to learn.

Chapter 2 Main Points
The Clueless Emperor Profile

- Clueless Emperors use their power in foolish and selfish ways.
- Behaving like a Clueless Emperor is usually a temporary affliction.
- A few people behave like Clueless Emperors a lot of the time.
- When a Clueless Emperor doesn't negatively affect you or people with whom you're aligned, it's advisable to walk away.
- The main goal is to overcome Clueless Emperors, not cure them.
- Stop colluding with Clueless Emperors and start overcoming. Be a Clueless Emperor Buster.
- Individuals with behavioral skills have a good chance of overcoming Clueless Emperors.
- Some Clueless Emperors are very dangerous, so trying to overcome them without help is risky.
- A group of people with behavioral skills who band together have an excellent chance of overcoming Clueless Emperors.

"Not to sound defensive [ahem], but I wasn't a Clueless Emperor all the time. I'd like to think I was quite charming upon occasion."
—A Recovering Clueless Emperor

Content and Form

*"When form predominates, meaning is blunted....
When content predominates, interest lags."*
—Paul Rand

How can a person who is targeted by Clueless Emperors succeed in a conflict? If you have struggled to survive their attacks, it's probably because important provisions are missing from your communication first-aid kit. When you've upset them and adrenaline is pumping, although it may seem counterintuitive, employing Clueless Emperor tactics won't help. Remember, it's their power that helps them win, not their wits. Without the authority to overcome them, you'll need other intelligent means.

Intelligence comes in several varieties, and many scientists and psychologists have researched, analyzed, and theorized about its complex elements. We can keep it simple and focus on the two types of intelligence that provide the best advantage for overcoming Clueless Emperors:

1. Analytical intelligence (IQ) helps people absorb information and think logically—it's innate and unchangeable. This ability is the source of the "hard skills" that drive content. IQ doesn't guarantee winning results, but it's an important factor in achieving success.
2. Emotional intelligence (EQ) helps people *convey* content

in a way that builds relationships—it's *not* innate, and can be learned at any point in a person's life. This ability is the source of the "soft skills" that drive form—whether through speaking, writing, or non-verbal means. EQ doesn't guarantee winning results, but it's an important factor in achieving success.

The first step to overcome Clueless Emperors is an uncomplicated but important one: it's having a clear understanding of these two types of intelligence—how they individually contribute to all communication, and how they differ. Whether it's content (achieved through IQ) or form (achieved through EQ) that more likely predicts success has been argued for a long time, but I don't take sides in that debate. The advice and recommendations in this book assume they're equally important.

Our educational system, however, doesn't reflect the same assumption. The hard skills related to content are heavily weighted in most school systems' curricula. "Reading, writing, and 'rithmetic" are required subjects, but the soft skills associated with form are usually electives, if they're even available. This lack of education in behavioral skills virtually assures that form is the weak link in the communication-know-how chain. As a natural consequence of imbalanced instruction, people commonly make more mistakes with *how* they present their content than on the content itself. Western culture's obsessive focus on content causes most people to ignore their behavior altogether—form often becomes nothing more than the unconscious and spontaneous mechanism people use to transport what's inside their heads—so they're ignorant about how powerful behavior can be, for good or ill.

Even though the origin of Clueless Emperors' ignorance differs from that of their victims, it's important to remember that victims are clueless as well. The Emperors' deeply ingrained selfishness is what makes them clueless, but their victims aren't aware that good form can compensate for a lack of power. Without an effective physical presence they lose—and they don't understand why. It's the underlying truth of the adage, "It's not *what* you say, it's *how* you say it."

Most often, the form people demonstrate is limited to habits that have developed along the way through life experience, beginning with early childhood. How skilled were your first role models in demonstrating and teaching these behaviors? Don't feel deprived if you didn't get adequate instruction in this area. The fact that so many people missed out on any kind of practical education on form is a common cause of failed communication. Bad form on the part of their challengers gives Clueless Emperors a significant advantage in any conflict. Their form isn't necessarily any better, but their power compensates for that deficiency. On the flip side, challengers who have good form use it to their advantage—they know it compensates for a lack of power.

It's important to develop effective form so the content of your message isn't ignored, distorted, or killed. In other words, the material presented here assumes your education and training have provided a sufficient foundation for critical thinking and problem-solving (driven by IQ), but you need education and training in the how-to-show-good-form department (driven by EQ).

Achieving effective form improves the chances of successfully communicating the information and knowledge inside your head. When content is strong but form is weak, it doesn't matter how great an idea may be—the communication will likely fail. Lots of good ideas get lost through inadequate presentation, and there are plenty of stories about such failures in these pages. Here is the irony of the content-and-form world:

- The better the form, the less we notice it—and content shines through.
- The worse the form, the more we notice it—and content is lost.

If you're thinking that achieving great form is more easily said than done, you would be right. When Clueless Emperors are blocking the way, maintaining effective form is an especially challenging task—the adrenaline rush from the stress often triggers inappropriate form—and the person holding the royal flush will always win the hand. It doesn't matter whether luck of the draw played a part.

Disagreements don't always lead to unsettled conflict, but when they do, expertise is required. Many professional resources in the marketplace tell us how to resolve differences, but most how-to-manage-conflict advice doesn't take power differences into account—and that's especially important if the person lacking power is you. It's not hard to imagine that power inequity is a significant factor when forecasting which side is going to prevail. Analytical intelligence and content knowledge as stand-alone advantages for the person with less power usually isn't enough to tip the scales—lopsided power triggers lopsided results—no matter where the subject matter expertise lies. When you're on the short end of a power imbalance and a conflict develops, Clued-In knowledge about form is required to even out the odds.

Regrettably, most of us don't even attempt to overcome Clueless Emperors—most often because we don't know how. The clout they throw around feels quite threatening—because frequently it is. The reason we allow them to prevail is that they have the capacity to hurt us in some way, and we fear they'll use it. We don't make the slightest effort to disagree, because overcoming them seems improbable, or even impossible.

There is a downside to this choice beyond the obvious "not a fair fight" element. When people do nothing to stop Clueless Emperors, the frustration that results can range from resentment to anger, fear, or even fury—and in the process, good ideas don't see the light of day. When people support Clueless Emperors to protect themselves, that doesn't work either. This choice can lead to guilt, loss of self-esteem, freedom, or in extreme cases, even life itself.

Let's hope you're persuaded to develop these skills and decide to make it a gift to yourself to learn them. To successfully negotiate with Clueless Emperors and be able to overcome them with effective form, it's crucial to understand these concepts:

- The nature of power
- The inner Clueless Emperor
- The gamut of Clueless Emperors
- The difference between behavior and perception
- The feedback formula that works
- The agendas of Clueless Emperors
- The effective use of emotion
- The advantage of awareness
- The behavioral skills of the Clued-In

These topics are presented individually in the chapters ahead, and each of them stands alone as an instructional guide. All of them together make up the formula required to stay ahead of Clueless Emperors. Managing the Emperors and getting your needs met at the same time may feel like an overwhelming mission, but that's only because you currently lack information.

Be patient as you read. The information is organized to teach simple concepts and skills that build on one another, with a focus on improving form, before presenting the full picture of how they work in combination. As a result, you may not immediately see the relevance of how any single chapter provides adequate clues to overcome the Clueless Emperors in your life, or how to recognize the behavior in yourself. Absorb the information a little at a time. Imagine that each concept and skill is a piece of a jigsaw puzzle. The pieces will come together, and the big picture will be complete by the time you close the back cover. Although it's true that learning to overcome Clueless Emperors is challenging, the trouble they cause can be overcome, with the right skills.

The information in this book also has a great side benefit: along with the ability to overcome Clueless Emperors when they behave badly, you'll improve your communication abilities in general—even if there isn't a Clueless Emperor in sight. There is everything to gain by learning the skills presented here, and absolutely nothing to lose.

Chapter 3 Main Points
Form and Content

- All communication is composed of form and content.
- Most people are better at content than form.
- Any inadequate form on your part is a calling card to a Clueless Emperor who wants to take something from you.
- Good form works with everyone, not just Clueless Emperors.

"I admit it wasn't nice, but when people lacked confidence and looked weak, they were mine for the taking."
—A Recovering Clueless Emperor

Power Plays

"The management of a balance of power is a permanent under-taking, not an exertion that has a foreseeable end."
—Henry Kissinger

What comes to mind when you hear the word *power*? People commonly think of power in its most conventional sense: hierarchy, control, or authority as it relates to a person's position, role, or occupation. Examples include the power of a boss, parent, teacher, airport security official, and IRS agent. Most of us are pretty good at respecting position power without much prompting. As an example, how would you respond to a police officer who stopped you for speeding, or answer the questions of a federal judge in court? Most people are on guard and pay special attention to their behavior when interacting with authority figures.

Sometimes managing everyday life interactions, however, isn't so clear-cut. We can't count on everyone with power to wear a badge or uniform that alerts us to the leverage he or she has. Knowing how to behave, and with whom, can get complicated. You may be thinking, *Doesn't it just make sense to disregard power altogether and just be pleasant with everyone?* Although this is well-intentioned advice, it isn't a realistic plan, especially with Clueless Emperors. When people misuse power and take advantage of others, being "pleasant" doesn't usually work with them, even though we wish it could. Skill is required in these situations, because Clueless Emperors don't respond very well to "pleasant." That's why it's important to pay attention to power dynamics when misconduct is taking place, and it's what this chapter is all about.

Although it's always wise to take position power into account, there is more to consider than rank alone. People tend to think of power in absolute terms, but another type of power can carry even more weight than a person's position: I call it *situation power*. This kind of power occurs when someone has a power edge because of a specific circumstance at a point in time. Position power alone is often enough to tip the power scale in an interaction, but situation power also has influence, and sometimes trumps position power. Here are some examples illustrating the strength of situation power:

- Police Officer Joe (*position power*) stops a speeder and recognizes the mayor's spouse (*situation power*) in the driver's seat as he approaches the car. It's likely Joe will treat this situation differently than if the speeder had no political connections.
- High school teacher Mr. Jones (*position power*) has a student, Betty, who has failed the final exam. Betty is the daughter (*situation power*) of the school's principal (*position power*). It's likely Mr. Jones will be extra careful telling Betty about her failing grade.
- Brad and Janice have been married for twenty years, and Janice has been a stay-at-home mom for eighteen of those years. Brad (*situation power*) is often verbally abusive and occasionally physically abusive toward his wife—always in private. No one knows. The few attempts she has made to address this with Brad have been met with fury. With no means of support, and the fear that her children would turn their backs on her, she is scared silent.
- Ginny's son is being bullied by her boss's son (*situation*

When someone needs or wants something from a partner who has more power, there is often a dilemma about asking for it. To personalize this, imagine a situation where your partner's Clueless Emperor behavior inhibits you from openly stating your needs. As a result, it should come as no surprise that your needs or wants may never be realized. When you have something to say, it's important to say it. Your partner might not otherwise know you're feeling unsatisfied. The first step toward positive change is for both people to engage in open discussion and overtly put power on hold.

Consistently failing to speak up, and caving in to your partner's every demand can lead to negative consequences. If you decide to change that dynamic, how competently you ask will make a difference. The person on the short end of the power stick can really benefit from effective behavioral skills in these situations. You'll learn how to do that in *Part III: Learning the Skills.*

When people decide not to ask for what they want and can let their desires go, by all means, they should do so and move on. But the letting go needs to be genuine. Sometimes people think they shouldn't speak up because their need seems trivial, or they may feel embarrassed to talk about a particular problem. Even worse, they may worry about being demeaned or belittled. The choice to speak openly is not always a comfortable one, but if people can't mentally dismiss their frustrations, the Clueless Emperors on the scene aren't going to disappear, and conflicts will intensify.

If your partner is a major-league Clueless Emperor who pretends to be unaware of your wishes or needs, it's helpful to go on record and state desires directly instead of hoping for a miracle to occur. By doing so, if nothing happens, at least you know it's time to devise another plan. When people are consistently reluctant to be direct, they irrationally build resentment over time, which isn't helpful to anyone. Remember, no one will know what's on your mind if you don't communicate. This driving force plays itself out in all kinds of relationships: boss/subordinate, husband/wife, parent/child, and friend/friend are examples. Even uncomplicated issues between people who don't see each other often can become grating. To illustrate, let's listen in on a conversation between two neighbors, Nick (who has a dog named Lucky) and Mark. As you read, decide which one of them is the Clueless Emperor.

Nick (*seeing Mark in his driveway*): "Hey Mark, glad I caught you. I'm going out of town again and hope you can watch over the house and take care of Lucky."

Mark (*hesitating*): "Uh, sure Nick. Always glad to help. When are you leaving?"

Nick (*not acknowledging Mark's hesitation*): "Tomorrow. I'll be gone for a week this time. I hope Lucky doesn't give you any trouble."

Mark (*hesitating again, longer this time*): "No, no trouble at all."

Nick (*not acknowledging Mark's hesitation again*): "Hey, great. Thanks. You've got the key."

Mark (*later that evening talking to his wife, Mary Ann*): "I have a major project at work next week and don't have time to take care of Lucky. I'm tired of Nick taking advantage of me whenever he leaves town."

Mary Ann: "Why don't you tell him?"

Mark: "Because I think it's important to be neighborly."

Mary Ann (*who has previously made it clear she's not her husband's dog-sitter backup*): "Well, I guess you'll have to figure it out."

Mark (*using a blaming-Nick tone*): "He really annoys me, but I don't know what else I can do."

This is a simple conflict between two neighbors, but it makes the point about what can happen when people let their needs go by the wayside. The house- and dog-sitting duties Mark has agreed to do for Nick in the past have now become Mark's burden. It will only get worse if he doesn't find a way to solve his dilemma. In this case, Nick is the Clueless Emperor because he has used his situation power (knowing Mark has pushover potential) to his short-term advantage. He doesn't realize, or perhaps doesn't care, that he's eroding their friendship in the long-term. Clueless Emperors commonly put their energies toward instant gratification without considering the results of their actions down the road.

Let's revisit these neighbors and listen in on a different conversation where Mark uses effective skills to overcome Nick's Clueless Emperor behavior:

Nick (*seeing Mark in his driveway*): "Hey Mark, glad I caught you. I'm going out of town again and hope you'll be able to watch over the house and take care of Lucky."

Mark (*knowing this moment would come and has prepared for it*): "Gee Nick, I'd be happy to if I could, but I have a really big project at work next week that'll have me all tied up. So sorry, but I won't be able to help out this time."

Nick (*surprised, and wanting to lay on some guilt to get his way*): "Well, that's a bummer. I guess I understand. I'll have to board Lucky at the kennel. That'll sure hurt my wallet."

Mark (*still prepared*): "You know, I heard Bill down the street has a son doing pet care and is charging a fraction of what the kennel charges. And Lucky would get to stay home."

Nick (*somewhat relieved*): "Hey, thanks man. I'm never home long enough to hear about these things. I'll check it out. Sure appreciate that you let me know."

Even though Mark had to do a little homework to find another dog sitter, the time spent was well worth it. He's the good neighbor he wants to be and neutralizes Nick's situation power at the same time. In this relationship, Nick's power comes from Mark's desire to help.

Uneven power distribution in professional relationships works much the same way. Imagine a disagreement between two peers. On the surface, a power difference may not be perceptible, but it's rare for any two people to be truly equal, even work colleagues at the same hierarchical level. As an example, one may be favored by the boss, have more seniority, or be viewed as a top performer within the organization. These differentiators carry weight, so it's unwise to assume position power alone is a sufficient factor when analyzing the cause of any conflict.

In social relationships, two friends may appear to be equal, but one may have done the other a lot of favors in the past, or have a special skill his friend often needs. They could be mutually connected in a network where a conflict between them would be awkward, so differences simmer and go unaddressed. Any lack of true equality—which happens rarely—creates a power difference, however small it may be.

It's sensible to assess an individual's power source and determine whether it's situational (usually of shorter duration), positional (usually of longer duration), or even some of both. The power quotient is most obvious when conflict develops with high-ranking Clueless Emperors. Everyone around these kinds of Emperors feels the challenge and is affected by it. Understanding the sources of power increases the chances for success in power-laden circumstances. The higher the risk, of course, the more detailed the plan must be.

A high-risk situation in a family unit occurs when threats of physical harm or abandonment drive victims of abuse into silence. The fear experienced by injured parties can be paralyzing, especially when children are involved. I'll borrow a popular phrase and offer this advice to anyone who has legitimate cause to be worried: "If you see something, say something." Any worries about making an incorrect assessment aren't worth the risk of saying nothing. As an alternative, discuss concerns with a professional third party for advice. Raising a false alarm is a better choice than remaining silent and discovering too late that your concerns were valid.

A high-risk situation in a professional setting might be whistle-blower information about organizational misconduct. Before that whistle is blown, a well-thought-out and carefully crafted plan should be in place. Many whistle-blowers have been sacrificed for lack of good planning on their part. Even significant information of wrongdoing in hand, coupled with a motive to do the right thing, is sometimes not enough to tip the scales in favor of justice. This is especially true when very powerful Clueless Emperors are the culprits—the consequences of failure for the losers can be heartbreaking.

Power can be as addictive as a drug. For many people, the more power they have, the more they crave, so care must be taken before disagreeing with them. People don't like to surrender power, no matter how intelligent or strategic it may be to do so.

Consider the example of the auto industry's "Big Three" CEOs (from Ford, General Motors, and Chrysler) after their doomed trip to Washington, D.C., in November 2008 when they asked Congress for taxpayer bailout money—each of them taking his own private jet to get there. The negative reaction to their arrogance was consistent from members of Congress to citizens on the street: *go sell your jets, then come talk to us* was the public response. To make matters worse, it was later reported that the executives had considered the possibility that their three-private-jets mode of travel might be viewed unfavorably by the decision-makers in Washington, much less the public (*d'ya think?*), but they chose to use their private corporate planes anyway.

This behavior is just like the emperor in Hans Christian Andersen's fairy tale (Appendix A) who carried on with the parade, even after he realized that he was publicly prancing in his underwear. The three auto executives traveled by car on their next trip to Washington, but the damage to their reputations and companies was already done. The bailout money General Motors and Chrysler received (Ford chose not to take any taxpayer money), despite their behavior, came with a fair amount of public animosity. One might legitimately wonder how many people didn't buy American cars during that time frame because of it. It may be true that knowledge is power, but it's usually gained slowly over time. The power of ignorance can kill instantly, so be emotionally intelligent and use your ability to influence respectfully.

Chapter 4 Main Points
Power Plays

- Power can arise from a situation as well as from a person's position or role.
- Position power usually carries more weight than situation power.
- Situation power occasionally trumps position power.
- Power is rarely distributed equally in relationships.
- The more power Clueless Emperors have, the better the planning must be to overcome them.

"I used to be king of my castle and all the people in it; now I'm just the king of myself—which is plenty good enough."
—A Recovering Clueless Emperor

The Clueless Emperor Inside You

"I have never met anybody who wasn't against war. Even Hitler and Mussolini were, according to themselves."
—Sir David Low

Using the skills taught here in a responsible way helps achieve Clued-In status. Readers who act on the information in this book will be more convincing, regardless of their motives. Exploiting the skills for personal gain at others' expense is what Clueless Emperors would do. How will you ensure your new skills are used for worthy purposes?

Consistently exercising power wisely is not for sissies. It's very easy to get carried away—when we're getting our way. Distinguishing between right and wrong in these circumstances is not always easy. But grappling with the misuse of power, whether it's our own or someone else's, is a responsibility Clued-In citizens take seriously. We've already learned how often people behave like Clueless Emperors. As a reminder:

1. No one is a Clueless Emperor all the time.
2. Some people are Clueless Emperors a lot of the time.
3. All of us are Clueless Emperors some of the time.

If you can't recall having an encounter with an Emperor, your environment would be an exceptional one. It's hard to imagine a Clueless-Emperor-Free world. Of course it's possible you don't notice them because *you* might be the root cause of other people's miseries more often than not and don't have a clue. It's what this chapter is all about.

We all behave in selfish or foolish ways on occasion. To err is human, as Alexander Pope so aptly said. If you commit violations more frequently than the average citizen, however, it's time to reform. Life gets easier when infractions are kept to a minimum—so let's hope your sensible, logical, and practical side is open to that possibility. This chapter provides information about the Clueless Emperor who inhabits your brain. Yes, all of us have one in residence. It's just a matter of how often that inner shark is let out of its cage to hunt for prey. It's essential to learn the signs of this behavior, and what can be done to resist any impulse to behave irresponsibly—the useful self-management techniques described here can keep you safe from after-the-fact pangs of remorse. When your inner Clueless Emperor shows up and shamelessly begs you to play in the water with the sharks, you will have the common sense to steadfastly remain on shore.

I don't know how often you behave like a Clueless Emperor, but your family, friends, and colleagues do know. When you act like one, they talk about it behind your back. Especially if you behave this way often, it's time to get Clued-In. If someone has encouraged you to read this book, consider taking it personally. It's incredibly easy to justify our own Clueless Emperor behavior—the human mind does a fabulous job of rationalizing misconduct to prevent any don't-even-think-about-it warnings from reaching a conscious level. The five questions that follow are designed to help raise awareness, so a cluelessness alert can penetrate whatever self-protection wall of denial you may have built. Be tough on yourself when answering how you interact with others:

1. Is it difficult to carefully listen to people who disagree with what you believe?
2. Can you modify your thinking when presented with convincing data that contradicts what you thought you knew for sure?
3. Is it challenging to remain calm, poised, and persuasive when discussing your opinions with people who don't like your ideas?
4. Do you ignore the possibility that opposing opinions could each be valid?
5. Do you *need* to be right?

Candid answers to these questions provide clues about your inner Clueless Emperor tendencies. If you're not sure how to answer honestly (take this confusion as a good sign—it's a step toward awareness), it may help to get feedback from trusted friends and colleagues. Be aware, however, if you behave like a Clueless Emperor a lot of the time, straightforward responses aren't likely. If you can't find anyone who will answer your questions directly, use it as a stepping stone toward self-awareness. To improve the odds of hearing the truth, ask people who have no reason to fear you, or to be deferential. Quietly pay attention to what they have to say. Discipline is key. Less talk and more listening equates to more learning. Defensiveness of any kind will decrease your chances of getting useful feedback that would be beneficial to know.

The ability to absorb and reflect on thoughts, ideas, and perspectives different from our own can be difficult when we're sitting in the power seat—but ignoring disagreeable information from those with less power, just because we can, isn't logical. Keep in mind that it's not a requirement to act on every idea or suggestion, but Clued-In people always make the effort to listen and consider a variety of perspectives. As Socrates advised, "An unexamined life is not worth living," so if you haven't done any examining before, now is a perfect time to explore your inner self. Failures and damaged relationships are fueled by Clueless Emperors who either don't know or don't care about the consequences of their actions. Their selfish focus blocks out feedback they don't want to hear.

Most of us would say there's wisdom in the "two heads are better than one" hypothesis, but sometimes our behavior isn't in sync with this principle. When we rely solely on our own thinking, the database for solving problems is limited to just one individual. It's human nature to give more credence to self-generated ideas, especially when the final say is ours alone, but the chances of success are usually diminished when only one person contributes. Self-awareness is a valuable tool when the inner Clueless Emperor shows up. If we're alert to his tricks, we can make sure his cage door is in lockdown position before any trouble starts.

Of course, mistakes occur occasionally, even without a Clueless Emperor in sight. Sometimes well-meaning people make innocent errors. In such circumstances, Clued-In citizens like to figure out what went wrong to avoid future mistakes—they don't blame Clueless Emperors who may happen to be in the vicinity. Although this can be a handy excuse when looking for a scapegoat, there are risks: missing information stays in hiding, and learning goes by the wayside.

Here's a way to differentiate whether missing information is the source of a problem versus the actions of a Clueless Emperor being the root cause: Clued-In people recognize when facts need to be gathered, so they do their homework and find them. Meanwhile, they don't pretend to know everything, blame others, or manufacture data in order to keep their momentum. If the blame game is going on, a Clueless Emperor is in the vicinity.

When you have the good fortune to interact with Clued-In citizens, please help them. Doing otherwise supports cluelessness. Inflated egos should never obstruct the discovery of pertinent facts. Business and government bureaucracies that slow down progress are notorious examples of this phenomenon. People like to complain that large organizations are the feeder pool for bureaucracies, but in reality, it's Clueless Emperors who are to blame. Organizations don't get bloated by accident. Bureaucracies are built over time by Clueless Emperors trying to outdo one another, instead of doing real work. When this is tolerated, it takes more people to get the work done, so Clueless Emperor Bosses have to add headcount. The new employees see what's going on and play the Clueless Emperor game to survive. This cycle doesn't have to repeat itself very often to create a bureaucracy. Never collude with this nonsense—neutralize the incompetence with your expertise instead. If a critical mass of people in any given system exercised their power sensibly, bureaucracies could not thrive.

Chapter 5 Main Points
The Clueless Emperor Inside You

- All of us are Clueless Emperors some of the time.
- It's useful to conduct a personal assessment to determine how often you behave like a Clueless Emperor.
- Do not use the nearest Clueless Emperor as a scapegoat when things don't go your way.
- Use your new persuasive skills responsibly.

"I saw myself as others saw me, and it wasn't pretty."
—A Recovering Clueless Emperor

The Clueless Emperor Gamut: From Blockheads to Bullies to Beasts

"There is no reason good can't triumph over evil if only the angels will get organized along the lines of the Mafia."
—Kurt Vonnegut

Clueless Emperors are not all the same. Because they have different levels of power and different kinds of self-serving motives, they wreak different degrees of havoc. Although the differences among Clueless Emperors are on a broad continuum, it's helpful to think of them in three categories to better understand their influence and consequent effect. For differentiation purposes, I'll use the following labels and definitions for these categories:

- *Blockheads* are disruptive and irritating (low level of power, somewhat nasty).
- *Bullies* are mean-spirited and ruthless (fair amount of power, very nasty).
- *Beasts* are menacing and dangerous (lots of power, exceedingly nasty).

These distinctions help clarify the variations among Clueless Emperors and how they differ from one another. The more power they have, the more damage they can inflict, so it's important to recognize their capacity to harm. As you become more familiar with how they operate, you'll also notice a direct correlation between power and motives—more power, more selfishness. Keep in mind that power by itself is not a bad thing. It's when it combines with cluelessness that we have to watch out.

As you plan a strategy to overcome a particular Clueless Emperor, it's useful to make a careful assessment of that person's clout. Understanding the Emperor's power source and selfish motives will help to calculate the potential damage if there is a failure to communicate. As an example, when first practicing the new skills choose someone in the Blockhead category where the least harm will occur if there is a break-down. On the other end of the spectrum, an encounter with a Bully or Beast requires a very careful approach. Jumping into a disagreement without preparation or backup is unwise. Better to jump into a tank full of sharks and end your pain faster. If a Clueless Emperor has more power than your skill set can handle, get expert help before proceeding.

Power comes from a combination of qualities or traits, and each one needs to be considered to understand a person's leverage. Following is a list of the primary characteristics that contribute to an overall power quotient:

- Intelligence
- Education
- Mental stability
- Physical presence and appearance (see specifics in Chapters 14 and 15)
- Talent
- Financial means
- Motive, drive, temperament
- Official role or position
- Political, social, and family connections

• A particular situation or specific knowledge that can be leveraged advantageously

When influential people also happen to be self-serving, these sources of power help to evaluate risk if we decide to openly disagree with them. When possible, it's better to have a thorough understanding of each power source (how intelligent? what is the education? who are the family connections? what is the specific knowledge?) prior to any conflict that might develop. It's too late to scramble for information when a conflict is in full swing.

Most Clueless Emperors are in the Blockhead category, which requires the lowest level of power to qualify. Because most of us behave foolishly or selfishly from time to time, and few of us have significant power coupled with purely self-centered motives, it's this kind of Clueless Emperor who shows up most often. The good news is that Blockheads pose the least danger and are usually the easiest to overcome with the right skills. They rarely become well-known, because as aggravating as they are, they generally don't have enough power to make news or cause major damage.

Blockhead behavior is quite common in situations where clueless people who normally don't have power suddenly acquire it for a brief period, usually through a short-term circumstance. They get so excited over an unexpected onset of control that the urge to squeeze every bit of juice out of their short-term reign is irresistible. The smallest advantage sends them on a power trip, and anyone they can hold hostage gets an earful about their extraordinary importance.

How this plays out in real life is exemplified by the story of the worker who gets yelled at by his Clueless Emperor Boss, enduring the abuse in silence. He needs to feel important somewhere, so he vents at home by yelling at his wife. She in turn takes out her frustration by yelling at the teenage daughter, who then yells at the little brother. The poor little kid has no power over anyone—so he yells at the dog! This kind of displacement is common when people aren't conscious of the emotional response to not having influence. They seize every opportunity to grab control of whatever short-term power situation becomes available. If they only knew how to gain the very influence and control they desire by developing the skills presented in this book. There would never be a need to "yell at the dog" again.

Just because Blockheads aren't dangerous doesn't mean they don't create stress. When a Blockhead causes problems, it's hard to be grateful the person isn't a Bully or Beast—but at least we know Blockheads can't destroy us. Some everyday examples of Blockhead behaviors are when people:

- Take credit for someone else's accomplishments
- Ignore customers
- Show up late
- Gossip
- Monopolize conversations
- Leave a mess for someone else to clean up
- Answer a phone call in the middle of a conversation
- Text in the middle of a conversation
- Don't follow through on commitments
- Don't say "please" and "thank you"
- Don't take responsibility for mistakes

A subset of this category is worth noting before we leave this group, because the behaviors are so common. Some Block-heads' misconduct isn't directed at anyone in particular, but what they do is irritating nonetheless. A few examples are when people:

- Talk loudly on cell phones in public settings (airports are favorite spots)
- Litter
- Take up more than their allotted seat space on buses, trains, and planes
- Push their way onto a train, car, or bus while people are trying to get off
- Butt into lines
- Deface public property with graffiti
- Don't watch where they're walking and bump into other pedestrians
- Block escalators, stairways, sidewalks, and intersections as if they own the real estate
- Disobey obey traffic laws
- Drive aggressively
- Use their car horns to communicate overall displeasure with the world
- Take up two parking spaces with one car

No doubt you can add some grievances of your own to this list—the possibilities are endless. Blockheads who commit violations like these can be tricky to confront, possibly even dangerous when you don't personally know them—they may be sharks in disguise, ready to bite if their misconduct is pointed out.

Even though everything in this book is geared toward reaching satisfactory results through skillful interaction, for this sub-category of Blockheads I'm suggesting a different approach. It might be best to leave them alone for safety reasons: who knows how they'll respond? If the bad behavior in question is truly posing a difficulty (keep in mind, you'll probably never see these people again), you may want to say something about their Blockhead misdemeanors. If so, please remember that any abrupt or demeaning tone on your part could aggravate the situation, so behave accordingly.

Here's a personal example of a possible way to handle this type of situation: I was at a movie and trying to enjoy it, but the person in front of me was vigorously texting. It went on for several minutes, and the light on her cell phone was taking my attention away from the film. It was impossible to ignore the distraction. The theater was full, so changing seats wasn't an option. It seemed that addressing the problem directly was the only realistic choice—I leaned forward and said quietly—and pleasantly—that the light on her cell phone was catching my eye. To her credit, she quickly turned it off. To my credit, I said it gently and chose my words carefully, making it easy for her to respond positively. Each situation with these types of Blockheads needs a thoughtful approach, so plan carefully if you decide to say something.

Lots of Blockheads are out and about in the real world, so the problems they present are varied and plentiful. The infractions they commit are usually related to lack of awareness or thoughtlessness rather than willful harm, so it's possible that effective interventions could help them see the error of their ways and encourage new behavior. A good reason to learn the skills.

The next category, Bullies, are another story altogether. Clueless Emperors in this group cause significantly more damage than Blockheads. Sometimes Bullies make national news, especially when they're famous. No profession is immune: Bobby Knight (basketball coach), Mel Gibson (actor), Leona Helmsley (hotelier), Al Dunlap (CEO), Larry Summers (university president and Secretary of the Treasury of the United States), and Anna Wintour (magazine editor) are iconic examples.

The Bully behavior of a well-known politician surfaced in the national news in 2007: John Edwards' extramarital affair during his United States presidential campaign. As bad as the negative publicity was for him, the exposé was only the beginning of his problems. The story evolved into a sex scandal with accusations that campaign funds had been used to keep his affair quiet. Edwards was universally condemned by the press and voters alike for his response to the allegations against him. He may not have broken any laws as determined by the court system (his indictment ended in a mistrial), but public consensus was that he had broken the rules of civility, and Edwards' life in politics was finished.

Most Bullies aren't famous, so their transgressions aren't well-known. Only their victims know—and anyone those victims choose to tell. Some everyday examples of Bully behavior—with varying levels of effect—might be a boss who threatens an employee's livelihood by engaging in unfair treatment, a colleague who damages a coworker's reputation by undermining that person's work, a friend who spreads rumors or doesn't keep confidences, a life partner who cheats, parents who withhold praise and affection from their children, and *anyone* who is verbally abusive. Bullies are intimidating and can potentially hurt us if we disagree with them or stand up to them—so the behavioral skill to assert ourselves is crucial.

The Bully factor has reached newsworthy status in work environments over the past few years. As an example, *Bloomberg BusinessWeek* (November 26–December 2, 2012) reports that the Workplace Bullying Institute (WBI) in Bellingham, Washington, has thirty-six state chapters with ten thousand people on its mailing list. The article goes on to state that the WBI makes a distinction, as does this book, between someone who is just plain mean (that would be a Blockhead) and someone who threatens, humiliates, or intimidates (a Bully by anyone's definition). "In the corporate world, bullying tends to be about power, control, and career advancement," the article states, but it warns that courts consistently rule in *favor of bully behavior* because employment laws tend to *favor employers' rights* over individual rights.

Even so, there is still an incentive for companies to enforce anti-bullying measures. The article goes on to say, "According to a landmark 2008 Gallup Poll of more than 1 million workers, the most common reason for quitting a job: an overbearing boss." If doing the right thing doesn't sufficiently motivate employers to discourage bullies in the workplace, perhaps the cost of replacing good workers who resign might do the trick.

The following example shows how Bullies can show up when least expected, and why having good form to fend them off is advantageous. To set the stage for the story, meet Scott, an architect specializing in restaurant design. He is a well-known expert in his field and valued by his customers and colleagues. Besides his day job, he also writes monthly articles for restaurant-industry trade magazines, and has done so for twenty-plus years. Consequently, he's often on the lookout for topics and trends that will appeal to readers of the trade publications he writes for.

On a trip to Europe a few years ago, Scott came across an international fast food restaurant offering reusable drink tumblers as an option—if customers returned the glasses at the end of their meal, they got change back for their effort. This recycling initiative reminded him of the container deposit legislation passed in some areas of the United States, and he thought it was a creative application for the restaurant industry. He met with the restaurant manager to get background and details about their process and found an enthusiastic colleague who believed that sustainability was the next big thing. Scott himself was an early supporter of the movement, and he was impressed by the ahead-of-the-curve approach this international fast food chain was taking in Europe. *Why not at home?* he thought.

The next month, Scott decided to write an article promoting reusable tableware in place of disposable products. He showcased the fast food chain in Europe as an example of a successful early adopter. Even though the sustainability movement in the United States was just getting started, and Scott's recommendations were novel, one of his publishers accepted the piece, and it was set for distribution the following month. So far, so good. Here's what happened right after the article went public:

Within hours of distribution, Scott received a call from an attorney representing a large U.S. manufacturer of disposable dishware who didn't take long to get to the point. The lawyer, citing the article, threatened Scott's health if he ever again spoke or wrote publicly on the benefits of reusable tableware! Scott was noticeably emotional when he told me the story, even though the menacing phone call had taken place years before. I had seen my share of bullying over the years, but this story was amazing—and Scott wasn't finished telling it.

A few weeks after this threatening incident, he attended a charity event where he was seated next to an editor of a highly respected U.S. newspaper with international circulation. As they were chatting, Scott mentioned the life-threatening warning he had received, and asked the editor about her experience with this kind of bullying in the newspaper industry. Her response: threats from the paper's disgruntled advertisers—who didn't like articles they believed diminished or challenged their brands—were so common, the newspaper had a dedicated security team to deal with the problem. She said the stress really got to her at times, but the newspaper's management team was sensitive to safety concerns and did what they could to protect their employees.

The moral of this story is that Bullies can turn up anywhere—who knew that disposable dishware and newspaper articles had such divisive potential? Unfortunately, Bullies don't wear identification tags, so we know them only by their behavior, sometimes too late. The good news for Scott is that he effectively handled the warning he received—he kept his cool, reported the incident to the magazine's publisher, continued to advocate for the green movement and, contrary to the threat jeopardizing his physical condition, remains in good health today.

Clueless Emperors who try to bully their adversaries into submission, no matter whether the threats seem serious at the time, should not be taken lightly. We may not immediately recognize how quickly a situation can become dangerous, so it's wise to be vigilant. Thankfully, in this case, Scott had the position power and skill to overcome the Clueless Emperor Bully attempting to block his path.

Clueless Emperors in the Beast category are the most dangerous. They often make international news because they use their tremendous power and ruthless ambition to inflict devastating, life-altering destruction. They're usually sociopaths or psychopaths who, in their own distorted minds, are merely doing what needs to be done. They appear to fully rationalize their bad deeds, and often come across as having no conscience. If you find yourself the target of a Beast, you need skilled support. People who attempt to overcome Beasts must be very competent and have plenty of power themselves. Some examples of Beasts include anyone who is physically abusive, executives who knowingly defraud shareholders, or government officials who disrupt political stability. At their worst, people sometimes die as a result of what a Beast does, as exemplified by Adolf Hitler.

A recent and well-known Beast is Bernie Madoff, the financier who swindled thousands of his clients out of many billions of dollars in a Ponzi scheme. The Securities and Exchange Commission (SEC) repeatedly received credible data about his illegal behavior over a nine-year period, but did nothing to investigate the allegations. To read more about this catastrophic blunder, read *No One Would Listen: A Financial Thriller*, by Harry Markopolos (John Wiley & Sons, 2010). It's an amazing story confirming the SEC obviously had Clueless Emperors of its own. It's hard to believe Madoff perpetrated his scheme when accurate and reliable information was steadily being supplied to the SEC for almost a decade before he was caught, but the reality is he did. Predators like Madoff can thrive only if we let them. People who turn their backs when they're in a position to make a difference like the high-ranking officials at the SEC did—jeopardize the lives of Clueless Emperors' victims.

History has shown that power out of control has crippled civilizations. Tyrants like Ivan the Terrible, Joseph Stalin, Kim Il-Sung, Saddam Hussein, and Osama bin Laden are examples of Beasts whose cruelties ended millions of lives. Attempts to overcome hostile oppressors have proved to be never-ending challenges throughout the ages.

Even though it can be tempting to get caught up in the frenzy of a power struggle—if you're in such a situation, take a deep breath and step back to analyze the problem from an objective point of view instead. Many thoughtful and intellectual scholars have done just that. For example, in 1887, Lord Acton, a British historian and moralist, wrote a letter to Bishop Mandell Creighton about their disagreement over power concerns within the Catholic church. A famous and often quoted portion of Lord Acton's letter reads:

"Power tends to corrupt; absolute power corrupts absolutely. Great men are almost always bad men, even when they exercise influence and not authority: still more when you superadd the tendency or certainty of corruption by full authority."

For our analytical purposes here, the specific issue these

two nineteenth-century scholars disagreed about isn't material. Our focus will be on the broader premise that power has historically been recognized as a problem and will, by its nature, consistently be a force of evil.

The first sentence of Lord Acton's quotation is often quoted and popularly understood. The second sentence, although less famous, also makes an interesting observation. Was he correct when he said great (meaning powerful) men (meaning people) are *almost always* bad, and is it inevitable they become worse when they're given additional power or full authority? Although there are exceptions to this generalization (consider Mahatma Gandhi, Mother Teresa, and the Dalai Lama), human nature and historical evidence indicate we should not be surprised that powerful people abuse their authority and cause distress or suffering for others. We should also not be surprised when any additional power they acquire brings about additional strife.

Of course, the best outcome would be to catch Clueless Emperors in the early stages of their development and help them see the light—or if that doesn't work, put them out of business as soon as possible. But there aren't enough skilled people around for us to count on that solution. *We can only dream.* It's why developing the ability to overcome them is the most intelligent course of action. Encouraging others to learn the skills is the next-best thing. Clueless Emperors can only continue to act when a critical mass of affected parties do nothing, or even worse, actively support wrongdoers for reasons of self-protection. Our choices when Clueless Emperors advance against us will influence:

- How they treat us—do we fold, or can we stop them?
- How the conflict ends for us—are we thrashed, or are we still standing?

• How the problem is resolved (success or failure?).

We must face them with our will, overcome them with our skill, or ignore them at our peril.

Chapter 6 Main Points
The Clueless Emperor Gamut

• The power of Clueless Emperors can come from any number of traits and characteristics.
• Clueless Emperors can be Blockheads, Bullies, or Beasts.
• If you want to overcome a Clueless Emperor, make a careful evaluation of his or her power—it's a critical first step.
• The damage Clueless Emperors do is often correlated to how much power they have.

"I straightened myself out before my bad deeds were discovered and 'escaped' jail just in time."
—A Recovering Clueless Emperor

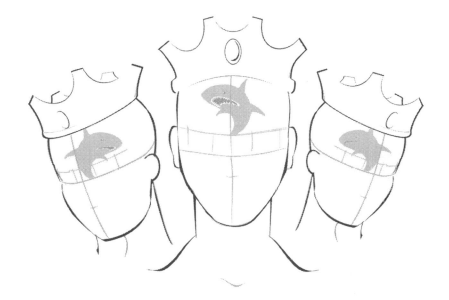

PART II
The Foundation

The Difference between Behaviors and Perceptions

"Facts are stubborn things; and whatever may be our wishes, our inclinations, or the dictates of our passion, they cannot alter the state of facts and evidence."

—John Adams

When Clueless Emperors attempt to halt progress—or worse yet, sabotage progress—we need practical strategies to get around their shark-biting ways. The physical skills you'll need to accomplish this are crucial success factors, but they are just the finishing touch. More knowledge is required beforehand. The information in *Part II: The Foundation* provides the fundamental building blocks for achieving the physical skills related to good form. With this underpinning, knowing the behaviors that best support intentions is easier to figure out. Let's get started by learning the significant difference between behaviors and perceptions.

To set the stage for this important concept, we'll need to return to the topic of content and form that was first addressed in Chapter 3, and expand on it here. As a reminder, there are two elements in every communication we send: the *what* (content) and the *how* (form). These elements are present in all spoken and written messages. An analogy might be a gift we give someone. The gift itself is "what" is given, and the presentation is the "how." Visualize putting a gift, price tag still attached, into a ratty old cardboard shoebox. Don't add tissue paper padding—to ensure that it rattles around inside the box—and present it unwrapped, without a card.

Now imagine putting the same item in an attractive gift box, removing the price tag, adding tissue paper for padding, wrapping it with paper and ribbon, and adding a card. It's the same gift, but the second presentation is far more attractive. This analogy helps us see how the two primary elements of a message work in much the same way:

- The "what" is the content (the gift), or the idea inside your head.
- The "how" is the form (the wrapping), or the delivery method, whether spoken or written.

If we could telepathically transmit our thoughts from one brain to another without talking or writing, a delivery method wouldn't be necessary. But that microchip hasn't been invented yet, so we have to create "packages" to get our messages out to the world, and these packages can take many different forms— it's up to us to choose which ones will serve our interests in the best possible way.

Many people believe the content of their communication is all that matters, but this commonly held belief is not correct. The package that carries the content of a message is crucial to how well that message is received. Does it succeed, fail, or fall somewhere in between? The delivery quality affects the clarity of communication, and influences whether we are viewed as worth listening to, or not.

Even though most people would intuitively agree this is a reasonable assumption, it's amazing how little attention is given to the *how* of communication. Not surprisingly, it's especially true of people with inadequate behavioral skills who are unconscious of their weaknesses. In other words, we generally focus on *what* we're going to say, and pay little if any attention to *how* we're going to say it. But we don't get better results by using the same ineffective methods over and over again, especially if people didn't understand our intentions or content the first time. This behavior is clearly unproductive, but it happens all the time.

It's strategic to give the *how* element of communication the rich attention it deserves, so our form is as good as it can be. The ability to maximize form will keep you from being trapped in the quagmire of endless debate when opinions differ, content isn't clear, or there is simply a desire to be more interesting or persuasive. The critical-to-know distinction between behaviors and perceptions provides the foundation for improving form. It's not well understood by most people, so if you know the difference, it will work to your advantage.

Behavior is experienced through the five physical senses: sight, hearing, taste, touch, and smell. Touch is used moderately in communication—a handshake, a bear hug, and an embrace are examples. Taste and smell are rarely used. Maybe unnecessary to say, but just in case, how you smell to others should be neutral to pleasing. If you're giving off any kind of unpleasant scent (too much cologne qualifies here), it doesn't matter what your message is. People will back off and won't hear a word you say.

The form (behavior) we use to communicate should be well-planned and deliberate, but people rarely consider how to physically present themselves. One explanation for this error is that most people are conditioned, through formal education and cultural norms, to rely on content as the primary, and sometimes only, vehicle for effective communication. Another reason people don't think about form is the fault of the human brain. Left to its own devices, the brain doesn't easily recall specific behavioral details. That's why it's common for people to dismiss the importance of how they are seen and heard—executing good form just doesn't make it to the top of their communication priority list.

Communication is dependent on form to relay content—there is no other way for the ideas in our head to get out to the world—but what we actually see and hear is almost instantly, and without much if any conscious thought, translated into perceptions. Even though the behaviors we literally observe may not be specifically recollected, the perceptions that our brains create from those observations stick like glue in our memories and are subconsciously converted to "facts." We make these kinds of inferences spontaneously and constantly. As a result, our perceptions (opinions or judgments) are more vivid than the behaviors that created them in the first place. This explains the phenomenon of how it is that several people, all viewing the same incident, can describe what they saw and heard in wildly different ways, after the fact.

Although the fast transaction from behavior to perception usually happens involuntarily—courtesy of the interpretive power of our brains—it's important not to confuse the difference between the two. Involuntary processing does not need to be outside one's awareness: your heart beats involuntarily, but you know it's beating. Simply realizing that behaviors and perceptions aren't the same thing opens up new ways of thinking. Our values, opinions, and beliefs are not facts, and we shouldn't ever talk about them as though they are.

When we understand that behaviors *are* measurable and perceptions *are not* measurable, life gets easier. Unfortunately, few of us know how to turn on the behavioral language switch when we should, so we argue unproductively by relying on our opinions. Most of us have never been taught to make an explicit distinction between behaviors and perceptions, so it's no wonder we confuse them—and it's a simple, uncomplicated concept.

Let's look at the mechanics of how this works. Of the five physical senses, we primarily depend on two of them—what we see and hear—to convey and receive most written and spoken communication. We *see* things like a smile, a raised hand, squinting eyes, a person's clothing, words on a page. We *hear* the words people say out loud, and the tone of voice and volume that go with them. These are sensory experiences, which means they're factual and can be measured. Conversely, perceptions are judgments we "invent" after seeing the smiles or hearing the whispers, and all the other behaviors we take in every day. Our perceptions aren't factual, and can't be measured. They are the *interpretations* of what we've literally seen and heard. If we can't distinguish between the literal and the interpretation, the perceptions of what we see and hear are easily blurred with content, and we potentially reach conclusions based on incorrect data: poor form gets equated with weak content and powerful form gets equated with strong content, when neither may be true.

A simple example: imagine a woman walking toward you, and as she passes by, you think to yourself that she's really good-looking. How fast is the transition from seeing the woman to thinking she's attractive? A fraction of a second is all it takes. Keep in mind, your perception that the woman is attractive may or may not be shared by others, but the physical description of her is factual (her height, weight, clothing, physical features, gait, and so on). It's important to fully grasp that our perceptions follow so quickly on the heels of our observations that it becomes easy to think of them as the same thing—when they are not. In this simple example, the woman is doing nothing more than walking by, and you quickly formulate opinions about her. Now add the complexity of verbal and written communication (ideas, concepts, or agendas) to the sensory input mix and pay attention to how busy the brain becomes, interpreting like mad.

Unless we're able to raise our consciousness and separate the facts from the fiction (our interpretations), all this brain-processing occurs subconsciously and very quickly. In these circumstances, the ignorance that follows can land us in some not-so-blissful situations. Think about how you privately assess people. Of course, other people are privately assessing you, and those assessments are based on a blend of form and content. That's why devoting the lion's share of one's focus to content, at the expense of not attending to form, is such a bad idea.

The quick interpretations the brain manufactures are actually great reflexes to have when our perception of a message is what the sender hoped to achieve. But what if the interpretations are not what the sender was hoping for? This happens frequently, and perhaps much more often than people realize. It's the lightning-fast processing time between receiving visual and auditory input and almost instantly creating associated perceptions that confuses this distinction. Of course, our perceptions are not facts at all, but we interpret what we see and hear so fast that we're lulled into believing our perceptions *are* the facts. Whenever people viewing the same event don't share the same perceptions, the stage is set for disagreements. Let's look at an example:

Rob (who has a laid-back and introspective nature) and Susan (who has an assertive personality and talkative nature) are traveling together. Their flight has been delayed several times, and the airline representatives at the gate are not readily supplying information. (I know, this is hard to believe.) Rob is OK with waiting patiently and has little need to specifically know what's going on. He trusts the process. Susan is annoyed, however, and has a high need to know exactly what's going on. She doesn't trust the process.

After seeing that the departure has been delayed yet another hour with no explanation, she approaches the gate agent. Rob can overhear Susan's exchange as he is sitting close by. When she returns, he looks at her and says, "Did you really have to unload on that guy? It's not his fault."

Susan is flabbergasted. "That's ridiculous," she retorts. "I did no such thing!"

It isn't important for our purposes to know how many people would agree with Rob's assessment of Susan's tone with the gate agent. Or how many people would think his choice of the word "unload" to describe that assessment was perhaps not indicative of his best effort to communicate. Of course, it's a very good bet the word "unload" (Rob's perception) doesn't remotely reflect how Susan views what she did. In the same vein, Rob probably wouldn't agree with Susan's opinion that he is "ridiculous" (her perception) for seeing it that way.

What *is* important for our purposes here is to be aware that perception-based, emotionally loaded words should not be stated as facts—Rob and Susan's exchange makes that abundantly clear. It's difficult to interact with people who state their perceptions as facts, convinced they're on solid factual ground, when in truth, they're on the slippery slope of their opinions. When people don't have a clue about the difference between their opinions (based on perceptions) and reality (the behaviors they saw and heard), there *will* be a failure to communicate. Count on it.

In everyday social communication—when differences of opinion or disagreements aren't looming—perception-based language usually works just fine. In fact, it's what our brains prefer to do. Think about what occurs when someone states a perception as a fact ("Bill is such a nice guy!" is an example) to someone who has the same opinion. Instant compatibility usually follows. It doesn't require much skill to be an effective communicator using perception-based language with people who think the same way we do.

Think about your position on some controversial issues such as global warming or abortion, and how you interact with people who agree with your views versus those who do not agree. It's when people disagree, feel emotional, want to be especially persuasive, or need clarification that the ability to shift from opinions to facts is crucial. The key is to know the difference between the two and never, ever confuse them.

Another reason to incorporate more behavioral language into communication is that facts are often quite compelling. As an example, which of the following sentences is more persuasive?

1. James careened recklessly through a residential neighborhood like he was on a high-speed chase.
2. James ran four stop signs while driving ninety miles per hour through a residential neighborhood.

The first statement is an opinion using perception-based words, and it's somewhat forceful as a stand-alone statement. It would probably make an impression on anyone who heard it. But the second statement, incorporating just two behavioral details (ran four stop signs, drove at ninety miles per hour), carries a bigger wallop. Do you see why the ability to distinguish perception from behavior is an important skill? It's the reason that hard facts are often more convincing than soft generalizations; and why knowing how to make the switch from perceptions to facts is advantageous.

Think of courtroom dramas on television or in the movies. Lawyers instruct witnesses to stick to the facts when giving testimony, and insist they report only what was seen and heard.

With few exceptions, opinions are not welcome. Subject matter experts may get paid for their perspectives, but witnesses are usually restricted to describing what they actually observed. If you've ever been in a courtroom (let's hope as a spectator), you know what this means firsthand.

In everyday communication, and for lots of good and practical reasons, people are more likely to use perception-based words instead of behavioral words in their conversations, speeches, and writing. Our brains are wired to quickly translate what we see and hear into perceptions, so we're on autopilot much of the time. For example, if a friend asks about a movie you've seen recently, it's far more probable you'll respond with a perception. You'll say something like it was "wonderful" (perception), or "OK" (perception), or "awful" (perception) instead of describing what you actually saw and heard on the screen.

We use perception-based language because it's easier and faster than specifically describing all the behaviors that led to our perceptions. These translations provide shortcuts to relieve us from needing to relate a bunch of details—it's an efficient way to get our ideas across to others. And that works well, so long as we're able to switch to behavioral language when it's important to clarify a message. Just remember, *behavioral descriptions are required if the content of a message is not easily understood by receivers, or differences of opinion are important to resolve.*

A good example of this occurs in the workplace when supervisors set goals and objectives for their employees. This is often a frustrating process, especially if *you* are on the receiving end of someone else's perception of what should be accomplished, because perceptions aren't specific. Almost everyone intuitively appreciates that people legitimately struggle with unclear, nonspecific objectives, but it's common-place in work environments for bosses to set objectives using vague and ambiguous (perception-based) words. This makes no logical sense.

For instance, the following words are commonly found in written workplace objectives: *teamwork, collaboration, leadership, empowerment, cooperation, critical thinking, problem solving, effective analysis, conflict resolution skills, customer focus.* And the list goes on. These are all nonspecific concepts based on perception. If these were the goals you were measured by, would you know how to achieve them? Will you and your boss easily reach agreement on whether expectations were met? If there are written objectives for your job, a review of that document will likely provide additional material to add to this list. If so, your objectives aren't going to provide any useful guidance, they don't lend themselves to measurement, and they won't motivate you to achieve them. Are you being held accountable for perceptions (which cannot be measured) or behaviors (which can be measured)?

Written objectives should require language describing the behaviors needed to accomplish them. If only subjective, perception-based terms are used, expectations won't be clear and disagreements between bosses and subordinates during performance discussions should be expected. Not surprisingly, these kinds of disputes happen all the time. When performance results are communicated in perception-based terms, they can be interpreted in different ways—sometimes wildly different ways—depending on who is doing the evaluating.

As an example, you may think a person who reports to you is customer-focused (*perception*) and approachable (*perception*), but your boss disagrees and says the opposite is true. Which of you is right? Without fact-based information, it's impossible to know. These kinds of disagreements often fester to the point where organizations themselves become the losers through lost productivity of discouraged employees not engaged in their work, because they don't get objective feed-back.

Job descriptions are also good examples of documents commonly laden with vague and ambiguous words based on perceptions. Examples include *strategic thinker, motivated, results-driven, team player, outstanding communicator, hands-on ability, capacity to multi-task,* and *approachable.* It's human nature for people to think they're a good match for any job they want to qualify for, and position descriptions written with nonspecific words make that easy to do. Job seekers who don't know the difference between perceptions and behaviors (that would include most everyone) won't understand why they don't qualify. These kinds of predicaments are common when perception-based language is the norm.

As an example, let's say "teamwork" is listed as a skill requirement on a job advertisement. The least-qualified appli-cant in the world isn't going say to a hiring manager, "I think we should cancel our interview because I'm not much of a team player." Specific skill requirements, such as "three years of accounting experience," are behaviorally based and more objectively assessed by the applicant as well as the hiring manager.

So how do people know if they're truly qualified for a job when a nonspecific description is the only guide? The short answer is they don't, and sometimes they file lawsuits citing discrimination when they're not selected, though this may be far from the truth. Even more important, how do hiring managers know how to objectively evaluate candidates? Many of them don't know either. Some companies use behavioral interviews, but even then, they're often not conducted effec-tively. The legal and emotional costs of these kinds of disputes are completely avoidable when behavior-based language is the standard.

When differences of opinion escalate, the human tendency is to defend our positions by relying heavily on opinionated language to make our arguments. Emotion intensifies right along with it. For those who haven't learned to make the distinction between behavior and perception, there is a sense of helplessness when Clueless Emperor Bosses appear on the scene. They thrive on nonspecific language and count on keeping the facts at bay. This situation makes it so easy for them to win. Along with most of the population, Clueless Emperors also use perception-based language much of the time. Most of them don't know any better either, but with the advantage of power, their lack of this particular skill doesn't change the results.

Management articles and corporate training programs that are loaded with perception-based language are plentiful which reinforces Clueless-Emperor-Boss behavior. Here's a snippet from an article in a highly-regarded international business journal that's intended to advise bosses how to instill persuasive skills in their employees:

Among the strategies, tapping into a social norm to create consensus is a powerful tool that gets people to follow the behavior of others. Managers should try to identify what the consensus view is in a workplace and think about what messages will convince others to join the consensus.

So what does this mean exactly? If you were given this kind of direction, would you know specifically what to do? Bosses who get perception-based counsel won't be changing unproductive behavior any time soon, which means the people who report to them are on their own. When coaching advice doesn't incorporate behavioral language, no one knows what's expected. The ability to maneuver a conversation toward the *facts* is what creates meaningful conversations. Clueless Emperor Politicians could take note here—more behavior-based language and less perception-based rhetoric would be appreciated by the people you represent.

Clearly, there is an important difference between behavior and perception. The simple guideline to follow when making the distinction is to determine whether something can (literally) be seen or heard. If so, it's a behavior. If not, it's a perception. The following quiz should help clarify the difference. Each of the words on the following list is either a behavior or a perception. Label each one with a B(chavior) or a P(erception). Answers are in Appendix B.

BEHAVIORS? ... OR PERCEPTIONS?

• Hard Worker	• Traveled to Texas	• Nice person
• Smile	• Sent an e-mail	• Responsible
• Cooperative	• Bought groceries	• Attended class
• Read the report	• Poor performer	• Certain
• Creative	• Made a sandwich	• Absent
• Pleasant	• Participative	• Silent
• Adequate	• Eye contact	• Quiet
• Arrived early	• Arrived late	• Sat down
• Won the game	• Walked the dog	• Effective
• Abrupt	• Friendly	• Waved
• Wrote a note	• Dominating	• Spoke out
• Supportive	• Top performer	• Treated fairly
• Expert	• Shrugged	• Said "no"
• Listened	• Enthusiastic	• Trustworthy

How did you do on this quiz? A tricky item on the list is "Listened," which most people would categorize as a behavior. It's not. It's a perception. If you made the wrong choice on

"Listened," see the explanation in Chapter 14 in the section on Silence. Remember, the general rule is when something can be physically seen or heard, it's a behavior. An *opinion* about what was seen or heard is a perception. Once you understand the difference between behaviors and perceptions, it's like riding a bicycle. You will never forget, and the skill to differentiate perceptions from behaviors will be yours for life.

Chapter 7 Main Points
Behavior and Perception

- Behaviors are seen or heard.
- The "how" of communication (form) does not get the attention it deserves.
- Our brains interpret what was seen and heard, and almost instantly create perceptions.
- People often think their perceptions are facts.
- Few of us have been taught how to distinguish between behaviors and perceptions.
- Behavioral language is required when content is not clearly understood by receivers or when there is a disagreement between or among parties.

"I want the facts, ma'am, only the facts."
—A Recovering Clueless Emperor Devoted to Dragnet

Feedback That Works

"Face the facts of being what you are, for that is
what changes what you are."
— Søren Kierkegaard

Although people are generally aware that feedback is a useful improvement device, most of them run for the hills when they hear the word—and with good reason. Skillfully delivered feedback is so rare that it's common, and logical, for receivers to be defensive when they get it. The intent of feedback may be to help us, but it usually does the opposite—and therein lies the dilemma. I'll take apart the mechanics of feedback in this chapter and show you how to give it skillfully and receive it less defensively—dilemma solved.

The previous chapter explained the powerful difference between behaviors and perceptions. We'll build on that knowledge here and look at a dependable feedback model that can be counted on to really work, almost all the time. What you'll learn is that behavior-based feedback encourages change, and perception-based feedback discourages change.

The initial obstacle for all of us to get past is thinking that feedback isn't worth the trouble it causes. The reality is that feedback can provide useful information if we choose to understand it—no matter how unskillfully it's delivered. On the flip side, it's important to take full responsibility for giving high-quality feedback when *we* are in the delivery mode.

On the surface, this advice may seem unfair. Why do I suggest that we gracefully consider all the feedback we get, no matter how revolting the delivery, but at the same time be accountable for skillful delivery to others when we're in the driver's seat? Here's why: while it's certainly possible to influence how other people behave, the only behavior we can completely control is our own. Paying attention to *all* the feedback we get is beneficial, because even a brutal delivery doesn't necessarily mean the information has no value. Calmly reflecting on feedback that comes our way, and being able to decipher it, can help us improve.

Feedback is most helpful when it's delivered as soon as possible after the behavior in question has occurred. Telling people what they could have done differently days after the fact isn't useful. People change for the better with timely, behavior-based feedback related to situations they can easily recall. Of course, this kind of feedback (versus the perception-based kind) makes change easier, so if you know how to deliver feedback effectively, there are big advantages for your receivers. And if you personally want someone to change fast, there are advantages for you, too. When feedback describes behavior instead of judging it, receivers are usually more motivated to respond favorably and act quickly on the suggestions they've received.

Clued-In citizens want to deliver high-quality feedback at all times, because they know a skillful delivery will improve the chances their receivers will understand and trust what they hear. Clued-In citizens are also realistic enough to know that the feedback they deliver might not get through—there are no guarantees—but they do their very best, every time. Delivering high-quality feedback is a priority.

Feedback comes to us through two means: directly, with words, or indirectly, with nonverbal behavior. As an example, let's imagine you're driving a car with a passenger in the front seat. As you approach a stoplight, your fellow traveler thinks you don't see it. The *direct* feedback approach might be for the passenger to shout something like, "Slow down!" The *indirect* feedback approach might be a grimace on the passenger's face, a foot depressing an "air brake," a thrusting of both arms toward the windshield, or a quick intake of breath.

Other examples of indirect feedback: someone frowns when disappointed, walks away when offended, applauds an accomplishment, or smiles when you've done something nice. People constantly give indirect (nonverbal) feedback through facial expressions, body language, and tone of voice—it's far more abundant than direct feedback. The behaviors listed in the Behavior Categories Chart coming up in Chapter 13 show the various ways that indirect feedback comes to us.

Although indirect feedback is more plentiful than the direct kind, it's also more subtle because it's nuanced and open to interpretation. Paying attention to it, however, is quite beneficial. We can't count on people consistently telling us what we may want or need to know. Clueless Emperors are infamous for their lack of feedback skills, so careful observation of their indirect feedback can be enlightening. If we don't notice their nonverbal behaviors, we're less likely to know how they perceive and evaluate us. An important step in overcoming Clueless Emperors is to be sharp-eyed and sharp-eared. Chapters 14 and 15 provide the roadmap for how to do that in a skillful way.

Direct feedback also comes in two styles, which I'll refer to as *formal* and *informal.* Both styles come in the form of words, whether written or spoken, but there is a distinct and important difference between them. With the formal style, we know beforehand that it's coming—even if the advance notice is quite brief—which makes it easier for us to take it in. If a friend says, "I'd like to give you some feedback," this is formal. When a boss schedules a meeting for feedback, it's formal. When a spouse says, "We need to talk," it's formal.

The informal feedback style doesn't make us aware that we're about to receive information in the same way the formal style does. It's delivered without any kind of advance notice and sometimes comes as a surprise. We have to be alert to pick up on it. Although informal feedback is more common than the formal kind—"Don't be late again" or "Don't worry so much" are examples—it's also more subtle than the formal approach, so it often goes unnoticed or unheeded.

Informal, indirect feedback is what Clueless Emperors are best at, because it requires the least amount of care and effort. Their aggressive behavior may have caused you to focus on self-protection when they're around, so paying full attention to their informal and indirect messages hasn't been a top priority. You must get past this course of inaction and notice their demeanor. Do they seem nervous, pleased, surprised, or perhaps aggravated? You need to know. If you aren't aware of the Clueless Emperor's behavior, you can't capitalize on the full spectrum of clues they're providing. If the feedback in front of your eyes goes right over your head, you've missed an opportunity to accurately assess your opponent.

The word *feedback*, as we commonly use it in everyday language, is assumed to mean that it's direct (with words) and formal (the receiver knows it's coming). The word *feedback* generally implies that something corrective is on its way. When people hear, "I'd like to give you some feedback," they're usually not preparing themselves for a compliment. The term *negative feedback* is commonly used in this context, even though—by strict definition—feedback can be negative, neutral, or positive. Skillfully delivered feedback that actually encourages change is atypical, which explains why the terms *feedback* and *negative feed-*

back have come to mean pretty much the same thing. So here is a big newsflash: feedback intended to encourage change does not need to be negative. When it's delivered in behavioral terms, it's easy to hear and can be a great source of development.

The reality is, the term *negative feedback* has earned its reputation in today's vernacular because feedback that's meant to encourage change usually doesn't work, so of course, it's negative. It hurts rather than helps. This usually occurs because the delivery (form) is sloppy, not necessarily because the content of the feedback is invalid. Receivers have little or no motivation to change, because the feedback is discouraging instead of encouraging. They feel frustrated or even unfairly "accused" when information is accompanied with shark bites. They won't understand the content because of the perception-based words, and may even be defensive or angry. That's a pretty good reason to call it negative feedback.

Imagine a different scenario: someone gives you feedback and uses behavioral language to communicate the message. Because it was delivered in behavioral terms, not as a perception or opinion, you will likely understand it, and know specifically what's being suggested. Behavioral language usually doesn't offend people, and negative perception-based language usually does. Behavioral words describe and don't judge. Some simple examples show this important difference:

A. "You're squinting your eyes."
B. "I see you don't believe a word I'm saying."

A. "I'm not sure what your tone means."
B. "No need to be sarcastic."

A. "What caused your delay?"
B. "Didn't anyone ever tell you it's rude to be late?"

Of course, it's unlikely anyone would label the neutral or behavioral descriptions in the "A" choices as *negative feedback*, because they don't make assumptions or pass judgments. It's why the "A" statements are likely to encourage a non-defensive response. Receivers are more open to change when their behavior is described rather than judged. The "B" choices do nothing more than elicit defensiveness and create bad feelings.

Skillfully delivered feedback is useful and can even be inspirational. In other words, when feedback that's intended to improve communication or encourage change is successful, it's not negative. I call this kind of feedback *developmental feedback*, because it reminds me to use behavioral words instead of perception-based words when I want to get my message across without triggering a negative response. When I'm in the receiving mode, I appreciate behaviorally worded developmental feedback, too. Who wouldn't? Very simply, the interaction between parties is easier and more efficient when behavioral language replaces negative judgments. It works like magic.

From now on, the term *developmental feedback* in this book means *feedback that is intended to encourage change, and it actually works.* Developmental feedback is usually constructed with behavioral language, which is why the ability to differentiate between behavior and perception is the focus of Chapter 7—it's a crucial skill. Look at it this way. Isn't it better to help people by giving developmental feedback rather than demoralizing them with negative feedback? Bottom line: helping people improve requires behavioral language, as opposed to perceptions or opinions that are not objective.

Let's look at an example of how a lack of feedback skill plays out in a conflict situation between two friends:

Kathy and Linda planned to see a movie on Friday night, but Linda calls on Friday afternoon to say she's very tired and asks for a rain check. Later that evening, Linda goes to a party to which Kathy wasn't invited. The next morning, Kathy is out running errands and runs into her friend Maria. During their brief chitchat, Maria talks about the party she went to the night before and mentions she saw Linda there.

The Unskilled Kathy can hardly believe what she's hearing and quickly interprets Linda's behavior as disloyal. She is hurt at first, then becomes increasingly angry. As her resentment grows, she starts revising history and imagines she has never really fully trusted Linda (emotions on a runaway train). She recalls occasions like this have happened before, but she had dismissed them. In the back of her mind, Kathy deep-down realizes she has no grounds for this kind of thinking, but it doesn't make a dent in her lack of objectivity. This is the kind of drama that occurs when people don't have the skill to manage their emotions.

When Kathy calls her friend and asks how she's feeling. Linda says she's much better, thank you, but says nothing about the party. The Unskilled Kathy—helpless at managing her emotions and incapable of giving developmental feedback—can't hold back and erupts with negative feedback: "You lied to me about being tired last night! I know you went to a party. I can't trust you!" The Unskilled Linda is now angry, too, and shouts back, "Hey, wait a minute, you have no right to talk to me like that!" And which of them hangs up on the other first is too close to call.

So what took place here? When Unskilled Kathy called Linda the morning after the party, she hoped her friend would be forthcoming with an explanation of some kind and offer an apology. When this didn't occur, Kathy behaved like a Clueless Emperor, using perception-based language ("you lied to me") in her feedback. Although she did offer up one fact ("you went to a party"), it was stated in an accusatory tone which couldn't outweigh the damage done by the negative perception that preceded it.

Whatever fleeting self-righteousness Kathy may have felt when delivering negative feedback to her friend, it certainly didn't help her gain an understanding of the facts. Her perception-based feedback was received negatively by Linda (no surprise there), so it didn't work. Of course, Linda didn't appreciate the words Kathy used, but she didn't have the skill to compensate. In this case, Kathy's information wasn't even accurate, but facts don't see the light of day when people are clueless. The average citizen doesn't respond well to negative feedback, no matter what the intent, or even what the truth of the matter might be. This situation is no exception. Let's look at how this conversation could have gone differently if just one of them (in this case we'll let Linda be the hero), had been more capable in the feedback department and used her skill to overcome her Clueless-Emperor-Friend's delivery:

When Kathy calls her friend and asks how she's feeling, Linda says she's much better, thank you, but says nothing about the party. So Unskilled Kathy erupts with negative feedback, "You lied to me about being tired last night! I know you went to a party. I can't trust you!"

"Oh," says the Skilled Linda, "I can only imagine what you must have thought. I'm so sorry you're upset. Can I tell you what happened?" Linda pauses briefly, giving Kathy the room to cool down and answer her question. "Sarah stopped by around 10:00 last night and woke me up." (Kathy knows Sarah and Linda have been friends for many years.) Linda goes on to say Sarah wanted to go to the party, but not by herself. Linda was actually feeling better after her long nap, so she told Sarah she would go, but wouldn't stay long because she wanted to get a great night's sleep. Linda finishes her explanation saying, "Sarah was OK with that, and I spent about an hour at the party. I'm sorry you were angry,

but I was telling the truth when I asked to change our plan. I hope if something like this ever happens again, you'll check in with me before privately deciding what happened."

Kathy is satisfied with Linda's explanation (*content*), and Linda's skilled response (*form*) has successfully diffused her anger. Kathy doesn't feel deceived, and the two friends plan to get together and see a movie the following weekend. If Kathy has any remaining concerns about Linda's trustworthiness in the future, it will be her responsibility to bring it up for discussion, and let's hope she uses developmental feedback the next time.

Developmental feedback instead of negative (perception-based) feedback may have strengthened a friendship in the second scenario. It also served the purpose of trading an explosive exchange for a calm and rational one. This is a common outcome when behavioral language replaces negative perceptions. If Linda hadn't spoken up, or if Kathy hadn't believed Linda's story, she could have decided to let their friendship cool, but in this case, it wasn't necessary. After hearing Skilled Linda's explanation, Unskilled Kathy felt satisfied with what she heard.

The challenges we face in building and maintaining trusting relationships are easier to handle when we operate from facts, which also makes emotions easier to manage. People respond better and faster to developmental feedback (based on facts) because...well...*it's not negative.* The tendency to confuse perceptions and facts never goes away completely, so we have to pay attention. The best any of us can do is be aware, and manage our inclination to make this mistake.

How can we switch from giving negative feedback to developmental feedback? It requires a conscious effort to identify the behavior we actually saw or heard that caused the frenzied sharks in our brains to think we could be convinced to go swimming with them. When we know what behavioral language is, and how it differs from perceptions, we can choose to use factual data (constructed from behaviors) in our feedback and coax those frenzied sharks right back into their cages for a time-out. Behavioral language trumps judgmental finger-pointing every time. As an example, think of it this way—would people rather be told they're rude when late for an appointment (*negative and perception-based*), or asked what caused a 30-minute delay (*developmental and factual*)?

If you've ever wondered how people would rate the quality of your feedback—and if you have not, it's time to start—ask your receivers, but be sure to ask in a way that indicates you truly want to know. If your request sounds rhetorical or challenging, the information you need won't be forthcoming. Remember, people on the *receiving* end of feedback are the best and only legitimate source to evaluate the quality of delivery.

Imagine how the dynamics of any system—whether it's a family unit (don't try this with young children—they will run you around in circles!) or organizational setting—could turn on a dime, in a positive way, if developmental feedback was a required standard. Picture a workplace or family that has the following policy: anyone giving feedback must ask immediately afterward whether the information was understood/accepted or not. Something like, "Was my feedback useful/developmental/clear, or unhelpful/negative/unclear?" are examples of how this question could be asked. The specific words chosen are less important than ensuring the receiver understands the message. Such a policy would also require that the feedback process couldn't end until receivers close the loop, which ensures a power balance between deliverer and receiver.

In a work setting, this strategy helps level the playing field between bosses and subordinates, which encourages teamwork and all but eliminates the chances of narrow-minded organizational arrogance. I know it's hard to believe, but some bosses give hit-and-run feedback that leaves tire tracks on their employees' bodies. As an example, many workplaces give lip service to the value of teamwork (*a perception*), without behaviorally specifying what team players actually do. With this policy in place, it wouldn't be acceptable for bosses to deliver hit-and-run negative feedback. They would be required to truly develop their people. Let's listen in on a workplace conversation between Sophie (the boss, behaving like a Clueless Emperor) and Chet (her subordinate) where such a policy is in place. Each of their comments is noted as either a perception or a behavior:

Sophie: "Chet, we need to talk. Your work just hasn't been up to par lately (*perception*), and I need you to turn out better work." (*perception*)

Chet: "I don't know what you mean. The quality of my work is the same as always." (*perception*)

Sophie: "Well no, it's not. It really has been deteriorating." (*perception*)

Chet: "Can you give me an example?" (*behavior*)

Sophie: "You were late with the financial report that was due last Monday." (*behavior*)

Chet: "But I talked to you about that ahead of time, and you gave the OK to extend the due date." (*behavior*) Don't you remember?"

Sophie (frustrated): "You said you wanted an example, and I just gave you one." (*The example is behavioral, yes, but it appears not to be accurate. By not disagreeing with Chet's account of what happened, Sophie tacitly concedes she had given Chet the OK. So her example seems invalid.*) "We're not communicating very well anymore. (*perception*) I don't know what else I can say, except to ask you to try harder." (*perception*)

Chet (dejected): "OK, I'll try to do better work." (*perception*)

Sophie: "Chet, was this feedback useful in any way?" (*We'll assume Sophie is required by workplace policy to ask this question.*)

Chet: "No, because I don't know what caused your concern."

Sophie: "Well then, let's schedule another meeting and try this again (*behavior*). Give me a couple of days to think of some examples. (*behavior*) Maybe that will help."

Chet: "Thanks. I'd like to understand what you want, so you'll be satisfied with my work."

This conversation has the potential for a positive outcome, because workplace policy required Sophie to ask Chet if her feedback was helpful or not. The actual words used in the question need to fit the context of the situation and are less important than making sure the question itself is asked. The workplace policy also holds her accountable for ensuring her feedback registers with the receiver, keeping her safe from delivering a Clueless Emperor Attack. She uses her supervisory position wisely to encourage clear communication. Let's revisit Sophie and Chet at their next meeting, two days later:

Sophie: "I want to help you improve your work quality, so I hope the examples I've thought of will help. I noticed at our last two team meetings the reports you presented had numerical errors that were pointed out by your colleagues at both meetings. (*behavior*) Do you recall that?" (*Asking for Chet's agreement is helpful here.*)

Chet (pausing to think): "Yes, I do remember. I was feeling rushed (*perception*) when I put those reports together."

Sophie: "Is there anything I should know that caused you to feel rushed?" (*Using a behavioral tactic, Sophie repeats Chet's words in the form of a question to get more specific information.*)

Chet: "My workload has been heavy (*perception*) since Steven has been out sick." (*behavior—Steven is Chet's best friend at work, so he's carrying the load on his own.*)

Sophie: "Are you the only one doing Steven's work? (*behavior*) I thought everyone was pitching in." (*perception*)

Chet: "Everyone is busy right now (*perception*), and I wanted to help Steven out, so I've taken on all his work tasks." (*behavior—Chet doesn't want to blame his coworkers for not helping.*)

Sophie: "Well, he'll be out at least another month, so I think you should delegate some of his work to others on the team (*behavior, although it's not the solution Chet had in mind*). I thought his workload was being handled that way, but obviously I was wrong."

Chet: "Well, I don't feel comfortable doing that myself. Would you step in and redistribute his work among all of us?" (*behavior*)

Sophie: "I'd be happy to, and I'm glad you let me know about this. Is there anything else affecting your work?"

Chet: "No, I think if all of us were assigned portions of Steven's workload (*behavior*), it would help me a lot," (*perception*) "but please keep this conversation between us. (*behavior*) OK?" (*asking for agreement*)

Sophie: "Of course. I'll keep it confidential. Thanks for filling me in and giving me the information I need to meet our commitments. Chet, was this feedback helpful?" (*The workplace policy question again.*)

Chet: "Absolutely. We got the problem resolved. Thanks."

Now the conversation between Sophie and Chet is productive because Sophie used behavioral language to lead the discussion. When people use behavioral language, their receivers are often subtly encouraged to do the same, and Chet is no exception. Notice this discussion between Sophie and Chet is interspersed with perceptions, which doesn't derail their conversation. It's fine to use perception-based language when it doesn't interfere with the progress of content. The goal is to use behavioral language to resolve a disagreement or clarify a point, which was the case between Sophie and Chet.

In their first conversation, behavioral language was necessary for two reasons: (1) they disagreed about Chet's performance, and (2) there was a lack of clarity—Chet didn't understand what Sophie wanted him to do differently. Their conversation failed because she relied exclusively on perception-based language, and Chet didn't have the skills to compensate.

In their second conversation, Sophie begins with a behavioral example of Chet's performance which encouraged a non-defensive response from him. You can count on behavioral language to out-perform perceptions every time. Continuing to lead by example, she adds specific behavioral information (two meetings where colleagues pointed out his numerical errors) rather than giving her perceptions. This tactic provides a model for Chet to follow. Notice at one point Sophie simply repeats Chet's words ("feeling rushed"), and then pauses. Her silence encourages him to keep talking, and by doing so, Sophie gets additional information: Chet is doing all Steven's work. When a speaker's words are repeated by the listener and then followed by brief silence, it usually prompts the speaker to continue providing information (see more on this topic in Chapter 14).

I hope you're thinking, *Wow, it would be terrific if I could give and receive developmental feedback instead of dealing with negative perception-based language.* If the workplace policy question seems artificial, it doesn't feel that way when it becomes standard operating procedure. Over time, it feels like a relief, because it removes so much anxiety from workplace dysfunction. Most new processes feel awkward at first, which doesn't mean they should be shelved. The workplace tension that can build when people walk around on tippy-toes for fear of saying the wrong thing all but disappears with this process. Not surprisingly, performance levels improve. I encourage the readers of this book, especially those in supervisory roles, to establish behavioral feedback as a standard. The results will be nothing short of astonishing.

A friendly warning, however: behavioral feedback is powerful and effective. In an office setting, poor performers who are chummy with Clueless Emperors in higher management may try to sabotage this process because it threatens their livelihood. If they have organizational support—and they usually do, or they wouldn't be around—they may try to undermine people who champion the use of behavioral feedback. Expect a negative response from poor performers when this process is introduced. Of course, this makes the implementation of a behavioral feedback standard slightly more challenging. New processes often face resistance—positive results make it worth the effort.

Ideally, if the leaders of an organization enthusiastically sponsor this policy, it helps ensure a successful implementation. Clued-In management makes a substantial difference. On the other end of the spectrum, if enough of the organization's leaders happen to be Clueless Emperor Bosses much of the time (especially when that group includes the top-tier executives), this strategy will fall flat and struggle to survive no matter how much support and enthusiasm there may be from the rank and file.

Brief training will be required to help users fully understand the difference between behaviors and perceptions. The feedback model at the end of this chapter can serve as a template for developing a short, two-hour module to get that message across. Once the process is implemented, team members will have an opportunity to improve performance based on clear, understandable behavioral feedback from their bosses and one another. If there are a *lot* of poor performers in a particular environment, some initial chaos will need to be managed, but consider how those employees currently harm productivity, virtually assuring negative business results. The upside of a developmental feedback policy is too positive to ignore.

How can poor performers be dissuaded from using this policy as a weapon—saying all feedback they get is useless— to exhaust their bosses and run them into the ground? Very easily. When disagreements between bosses and subordinates can't be resolved, a third-party mediator needs to step in to resolve differences. A competent human resources manager or ombudsperson can serve in that capacity. Over time, the consistent application of developmental feedback as the norm will create a culture where interventions for this problem aren't necessary. A critical mass of employees will develop the skills to self-manage and teach others.

What happens if a poor performer doesn't improve? Remember that even the best developmental feedback cannot cure every performance problem. If an employee who receives developmental feedback hasn't shown improvement over time, the result could be anything from a job change to a termination, depending on the circumstances. This is how performance management should work, though it rarely does. On the positive side, it isn't difficult to implement and reinforce the simple techniques required to raise performance. On the negative side, pushing through resistance to change can be difficult, so be prepared.

All too often bosses lack the skill to give developmental feedback and behave like Clueless Emperors instead; they weaken relationships by delivering negative feedback. Some Clueless Emperor Bosses just ignore poor performers altogether and give no feedback at all, which means other team members have to pick up the slack. Those carrying the extra load eventually become resentful, and the quality of their work may decline. Good performers often leave a company to find a better boss in these situations. In fact, statistically speaking, it's why employees begin looking for another job, as we learned in Chapter 6. Of course, the poor performers stay. This type of workplace environment is perfect for them. Organizations shouldn't tolerate Clueless Emperor behavior from anyone, but especially not from supervisors who are paid to manage and lead others. These people weaken trust and lower productivity through their clueless, inept actions.

It's not hard to imagine how a hierarchical chain of bosses who regularly give negative feedback can harm a company. A lot of them are out there. Unfortunately, this silent killer—the inability to give developmental feedback—is rarely identified as the root cause of a company's failure to perform. It seems hard to believe that organizations would tolerate productivity losses when such simple skills could change the equation, but it happens routinely. Their Clueless Emperor Egos get in the way. You can read more about this problem in Robert I. Sutton's book *The No Asshole Rule* (Business Plus Imprint, Hachette Book Group, 2007), where he presents many good examples of this organizational shortcoming.

If a company has an effective performance management process, where feedback skill is a requirement, there is no reason for anyone, bosses and workers alike, to have difficulty communicating about performance. In my experience, a lack of developmental feedback skill is why companies can't measure performance in the first place. Remember, perceptions can't be measured, and the goals and objectives of most companies are written in perception-based terms. When profit and productivity are declining, finger-pointing becomes the norm because accurate measurements to assess root causes don't exist. It's common for organizations to spend bundles of money buying or developing elaborate performance management systems—and change them every few years because they never seem to work—when the primary cause of their problems is a lack of feedback skill.

As an example, a midsize company would typically spend about $300,000 on a web-based performance management process, and that's just for the software. Employee education and implementation expenses are extra. Very large companies spend multiple millions of dollars on performance management. These systems are the Band-Aid, not the cure, so they don't solve the problems they were designed to fix. When this failure becomes apparent to users, it's not uncommon for them to get discouraged, which is why companies abandon their performance management process every few years and look for a better product to pin their hopes on—trusting that a new (and even more expensive) process will get the job done. They throw good money after bad without understanding the real issues. The pay-for-performance goal becomes a pay-for-perception nightmare.

During my career as a human resources executive, I've seen these cycles repeat over and over—large, sophisticated companies are no exception. I don't know anyone who likes performance management done this way, bosses and subordinates alike, but company after company follows this lemming-like approach to measuring performance. For those who appreciate the advantage that feedback expertise and behavioral language can bring, it's hard to understand how such ineffective methods continue to survive. The crux of the problem is that too few people understand the mechanics of behavioral language skills. It's like building sand castles and expecting them to last—ineffective construction material doesn't stand the test of time.

These principles also apply to non-workplace relationships. Family members and friends become vulnerable to failure when all they hear is negative feedback. If you want someone in your life to do something differently, give developmental feedback. As an example, "I noticed you didn't take out the trash, and I'm wondering what happened" will yield better results than "You slacker, you're so forgetful—I can never depend on you." Who wouldn't be deflated if that's the kind of language they had to listen to all day?

How do people commonly react to negative feedback? Well, not surprisingly, they get defensive and push back. Or they just ignore it. Plain and simple, negative feedback doesn't get dependable results. Fear tactics may drive compliance for a brief period, but they never encourage commitment. Any service industry that wants to improve the customer experience should take note here—employees on the front line treat customers based on how they themselves are treated by their bosses and colleagues.

As discussed earlier in this chapter, curious people who know the difference between perceptions and behaviors are able to self-manage the tendency to react defensively and even help the unskilled delivery person convert their perceptions into behaviors. Don't count on coming into contact with very many people who know how to do this—it's a rare skill. Being skillful yourself makes it easier to sort through poorly delivered feedback that comes your way and get at the nugget of the message. People with a genuine desire to improve know that feedback in any form is useful—if they understand it.

As an example, let's say someone calls you out for being judgmental, and you don't have a clue what the person is talking about. An artful response (to help the delivery person translate the perception-based feedback into a behavioral example) might be, "Thanks for telling me. I'm not aware of doing that and want to understand what you mean. Can you give me some examples?" Ask a sufficient number of questions to uncover the behavioral details that led to the person's perception of you. This is the way to help the feedback delivery person convert negative feedback to developmental feedback—it's that simple. Beats feeling discouraged, getting defensive, and not having a clue, doesn't it?

Let's end this chapter with a few comments about positive feedback. We know that feedback intended to encourage *change* works best with behavioral language. When feedback is intended to encourage *current behavior*, not surprisingly, perception-based language works just fine. People respond favorably to *positive* perceptions. Everyone likes to hear comments like "You did a terrific job!"

A positive perception that includes a behavioral example to support the praise further reinforces the receiver's motivation to continue. A statement like "Thanks for the research you did to answer the concerns of Customer Jones (*behavior*)—it was well done (*perception*)" will be appreciated. This kind of feedback is called *reinforcing feedback* and usually provides incentive for the receiver to continue the behavior being praised.

The same is true in personal relationships. Examples might be when a grateful dinner guest says, "Thanks for a terrific meal," or a friend says, "I really appreciated your helping me out when I was sick." These statements go a long way to show caring and build trust at the same time. The more specific (behavioral) the feedback is, the better the results will be.

The following chart captures the definitions of the feedback choices discussed in this chapter:

TYPES OF BEHAVIORAL FEEDBACK

Positive	Reinforcing
A positive perception	A positive perception with a specific example
Intended to compliment	Intended to compliment

Negative	Developmental
Usually involves negative perceptions	Usually involves specific examples/behavior
Intended to cause change but doesn't work	Intended to cause change and it works

Chapter 8 Main Points
Feedback That Works

- Developmental feedback is constructed from behavioral language and helps people change.
- Negative feedback is constructed from perception-based language and doesn't help people change.
- Feedback should be immediate and frequent if change is desired.
- Personal relationships and organizations suffer when negative feedback is the norm.
- Perception-based language should be avoided when feedback is intended to encourage change.
- Verbalizing positive perceptions is fine when giving a compliment is the goal.
- Positive perceptions with examples reinforce behavior.
- Behavioral language resolves disagreements and clarifies information.

"There is no need to run for the hills.
Developmental feedback will save the day."
—A Recovering Clueless Emperor

CHAPTER 9

The Harmful Agendas of Clueless Emperors

"A man should never be ashamed to own he has been in the wrong, which is but saying, in other words, that he is wiser today than he was yesterday."
—Alexander Pope

When people choose to speak or write, they're intending to convey information of some kind—an opinion, a directive, a request, a question, feedback—or sometimes a little socializing is all they have in mind. Whether we're speaking or writing, the task of putting words together to communicate an idea is usually spontaneous. If the transmission is successful, the sender's intention is rewarded when the receiver understands the message and offers a response in return.

Communication at its best is just this simple—a straightforward exchange of thoughts, opinions, or ideas. Subject matter is uncomplicated with a low-to-medium emotional threshold. I refer to this trouble-free type of communication as exchanging *viewpoints*, which can be accomplished by means of talking (social chitchat is an example) or writing (texting is an example). Clueless Emperors are relatively civilized and mild-mannered when viewpoints are exchanged, because they're not competing in this type of interaction and have no stake in the outcome.

Sometimes, however, communication gets more complicated, especially when multiple people are involved, issues are complex, actions must be taken, or opinions differ. If invested parties have different approaches to solving a problem, viewpoints often evolve into agendas. Various perspectives come into play, people sometimes get contentious, and the simple exchange of viewpoints becomes a distant memory. In these circumstances, emotion and motivation intensify.

Differing opinions that are openly discussed should logically encourage better decision-making, but all too often those differences become fixed in the minds of the invested parties. The longer the discussion goes on, the more fixed the opinions become, and people start digging in their heels instead of listening. In these situations, settling disagreements and finding good solutions is challenging.

Agendas are a normal consequence of human interaction when life moves from the slow lane of simple conversation to the fast lane of complex debate. Some people associate the word "agenda" with a negative connotation, as though something underhanded is occurring, but it isn't always that way. Agendas can have either positive or negative purposes depending on the people creating and defending them—are they clueless or Clued-In? Maria Bartiromo, television news journalist, had it right when she said, "As a reporter, I approach every situation knowing that everyone has his or her own agenda; it's not a bad thing; it's just a fact."

This chapter provides insight into why Clueless Emperors are the most difficult to overcome when they have agendas with negative purposes. Negative agendas occur in a wide variety of venues—from family disputes all the way to global warfare. Clueless Emperors' infinite capacity for self-serving motives shifts into high gear when there is any kind of disagreement with their agendas. The information here will help you understand how agendas get out of control when the human trait of liking-to-be-right metastasizes into its evil twin needing-to-be-right, and why we need to understand the difference between the two. Clueless Emperors regularly exit the like-to-be-right zone and head straight for need-to-be-right territory if their agendas are at stake. The following chart shows examples of how viewpoints evolve into corresponding agendas.

VIEWPOINTS	VS.	AGENDAS
• A colleague at work behaves arrograntly.		• An arrogant colleague is undermined by his peers to make him look bad.
• Your aunt gossips too much.		• Your family members try to convince your mother not to invite your gossipy aunt to family functions.
• An earthquake in Haiti will cause global economic problems.		• An organization is created to provide relief for Haitian earthquake victims.
• The football coach at your son's high school is ineffective.		• The parents of the football players have a meeting to discuss the football program.

Notice in these illustrations how viewpoints develop into agendas when a situation or plan gathers strength, and actions become a natural consequence. Also notice they can have positive or negative purposes. Whether agendas are developed for good or ill purposes varies based on the motives of the people creating and defending them. The amount of time people invest in an agenda often correlates to their drive and emotion—the more time they spend, the more personal the agenda becomes, and so the more tenaciously they're likely to protect it. When negative agendas materialize, we can be sure that selfish people are lurking nearby and putting pressure on people without sufficient power. "My way or the highway" is the goal, and those in command usually prevail, no matter what the facts are. Why does this happen? Because the people without power lack the skill to influence the Clueless Emperors who control the outcome.

It's beneficial to have a full understanding of why people develop agendas and how those agendas are viewed by those who don't buy into them, as well as by those who do. It's common to defend an agenda's validity by using the same logic that created it, but emotion also plays a critical role—even if that emotion only registers at a subconscious level. It's hard to grasp the big picture of any agenda without considering the purpose that supplied the fuel for its content. People don't create agendas like machines, presenting only hard, straightforward, logical data. Life would be easier if that were truly the case. As agendas are developed, defended, or disagreed with, they become increasingly entwined with emotion. This isn't necessarily good or bad—it depends on whether motives are selfish or selfless—but all agendas have an emotional component. And sometimes that emotion plays out in significant ways.

A horrific example of an agenda's emotional power occurred in 1986 with NASA's fatal decision to launch the space shuttle called *Challenger*. The Morton-Thiokol Company was a vendor to NASA and supplied mechanical gaskets called O-rings for the shuttle. Many months before the launch, several engineers at NASA and Morton-Thiokol knew the O-rings could potentially fail in cold weather—the parts would become rigid and lose the flexibility to seal properly. At the time, there wasn't technical agreement on precise temperature thresholds where this would occur, but anything below 40°F was considered risky by many experts. Perhaps not a likely weather concern in Florida, so it may have been easy for NASA management to put aside this information as the pressure mounted to stay on schedule.

The launch date was set for January 28 and despite the 31° F temperature that morning, the liftoff took place as planned. Shockingly, the long-held information about the O-rings' poor performance at low temperatures had never been thoroughly vetted. Those who knew about the problem, and had the authority to delay, chose to go ahead—even though several NASA and Morton-Thiokol engineers advised against it. News reports after the accident said those who were aware of the technical concerns—and worried about a mechanical failure—expected it very shortly after liftoff. They must have quietly breathed a little easier as the rocket climbed into the sky. And then, 73 seconds after the shuttle left the ground, a huge explosion tore the fuel tank apart—killing all seven people on board.

Many researchers have since investigated the actions contributing to the disaster, so ample literature is available that documents the events leading up to the tragedy. Roger Boisjoly, a Morton-Thiokol scientist at the time, was one of the first to expose the technical problem with O-rings several months before the disaster occurred. He sent e-mails expressing his concerns to people who could have done something. The information was ignored. Mr. Boisjoly didn't give up. He hounded and implored. He showed pictures of what damaged O-rings looked like after exposure to low temperatures. Mr. Boisjoly was not alone in his effort to convince decision-makers of the danger—several other engineers advocated right along with him. The information continued to be ignored.

In a dramatic gesture the night before the scheduled launch, thirty-four manager-engineers from NASA and Morton-Thiokol were called to a last-minute meeting to discuss the controversy over whether to go ahead as planned the next morning. Some of the attendees participated via teleconference. At that late date, there wasn't a unified position on the viability of the O-rings' performance at low temperatures—which was the primary agenda item for the meeting. *What? The night before the launch?*

Not surprisingly, there was discord among the participants that evening. Boisjoly was joined by several other engineers who pressed for a delay. There were many signs pointing toward canceling. To make a critical situation worse, the phone transmission quality during the meeting was so poor that some participants on the phone couldn't hear the entirety of the discussion taking place, though they said nothing about it at the time. *A last-minute teleconference meeting, lack of agreement on the data, some participants can't hear but don't say anything… and lives are at stake? What were they thinking?* At the meeting's conclusion, it's safe to say that none of the attendees believed there was a universally good feeling to go ahead the next morning, and yet that was the decision.

And the rest, of course, is history. In brutally graphic terms, NASA management risked seven people's lives for reasons that aren't logically acceptable. It seems impossible to imagine a desire to launch took precedence over compelling hard data that more than suggested a delay.

On the day of the explosion, of course, these facts were not yet known by the public. In an attempt to comfort a fearful nation reeling from the shock of the tragedy, President Ronald Reagan responded by giving a short speech from the Oval Office that evening and said, in part:

"*I know it is hard to understand, but sometimes painful*

things like this happen. It's all part of the process of exploration and discovery. It's all part of taking a chance and expanding man's horizons. The future doesn't belong to the fainthearted; it belongs to the brave."

This rhetoric raises some questions: Do we really need to accept that painful things like this will happen, despite available information that indicates safer choices? Does the process of exploration and discovery preclude a requirement to listen and cooperate? What level of danger should be tolerated as we expand our horizons? Why didn't Reagan withhold a rationale for the accident until after an investigation (which he later ordered) was completed? Finally and perhaps most important, is it brave to risk *other* people's lives?

Summarizing the events of a disaster can lead to over-simplification—a thorough analysis provides a more balanced and objective view. The Rogers Commission Report, created by presidential order to investigate the *Challenger* disaster, was presented June 9, 1986, and recommended several new safety measures for NASA to follow, including its organizational process of handling space missions. The investigators apparently didn't think that "painful things like this (are bound to) happen" as Reagan's speech implies.

In a separate investigation, Diane Vaughan, a sociologist and professor at Columbia University, conducted several years of extensive research, analyzing the events leading up to the accident. Her book, *The Challenger Launch Decision* (The University of Chicago Press, 1996), presents the decision to launch from a unique perspective. Vaughan's research indicated that the culture at NASA had evolved over the years to become so tolerant of risk that their decision to launch was an acceptable one, based on environmental conditioning. In other words, the organizational way of life at NASA caused the leaders there to become immune to warning signals that contradicted logic.

Is it possible that well-intentioned people can be taken over by cultural norms, so they shouldn't be held accountable for their decisions? Is this a credible way to rationalize the cause of this disaster? *More important, if one of these decision-makers had had a loved one on board the shuttle that fateful day, would the group have reached the same conclusion?* From my perspective, the answer to these questions is a clear and unambiguous "NO."

Although no one at NASA or Morton-Thiokol had evil-doing in mind, the risk-tolerant-culture theory just can't be supported, in my view. If so, there are many, many other catastrophes where cultural norms could be used as explanations for people doing bad things. Clueless Emperors misusing power and forcing a harmful agenda seems to be a better fit when searching for a root cause of the *Challenger* disaster. When individuals are not held accountable for their decisions, they won't learn as profoundly from mistakes, and as a consequence, more failures can and should be expected. It's why analyzing this particular tragedy is so instructive—there aren't any criminals to blame—yet people died because of excessive hubris. Maybe Clueless Emperors would exercise appropriate caution if they worked in a culture where mistakes carried corresponding penalties.

As often happens with whistle-blowers, Roger Boisjoly was praised by a few after the fact and had his fifteen minutes of fame, but spent much of the rest of his life paying the price for speaking out. He was rejected by many of his co-workers, and his company cut him from space work—a good example of Clueless Emperors exacting revenge when they lose. Mr. Boisjoly died in January 2012 without ever receiving the full recognition he deserved.

The behavioral skills the scientists exhibited in their effort to delay the launch is now lost to history. No video or audio recordings of their warnings exist. What is clear is that they spoke up, and the substance of their message had merit. Using content and form as a backdrop: is it possible they could have been more persuasive had they shown better form when conveying the content they knew to be correct? Was there anything they could have done differently to convince the Clueless Emperors at NASA to be more open-minded? Is it possible that these scientists allowed their frustration to have a starring role in their argument, and so became less effective at presenting their case? We don't know for sure, but chances are—human nature being what it is—there were missed opportunities to more skillfully present what they knew.

James Oberg, an NBC News space consultant, worked at NASA for twenty-two years and is an expert in his field. In an NBC News special report (January 25, 2011) commemorating the twenty-fifth anniversary of the disaster, he addressed seven myths related to the incident that he encouraged the public to remember in honor of those who perished. Myth #7, *Political Pressure Forced the Launch*, is worth special mention here because it shines a spotlight on the Clueless Emperor factor. Oberg wrote:

"NASA managers made a bad call for the launch decision, and engineers who had qualms about the O-rings were bullied or bamboozled into acquiescence. The skeptics' argument that launching with record cold temperatures is valid, but it probably was not argued as persuasively as it might have been, in hindsight."

It may seem unduly harsh to even suggest that these scientists be second-guessed about how they presented their data, but the reality is the only behaviors they could fully control were their own. A skillful delivery means we're more likely to influence change—those who oppose us are more persuaded to consider alternatives. This is a responsibility everyone should take seriously. The *Challenger* disaster is a chilling reminder that our ability to overcome Clueless Emperors has the potential to save lives.

Clueless Emperors routinely drive their agendas by refusing to consider other people's perspectives. While this is happening, the opportunity to find the best solution is lost, because it's the person with the most power who wins. Sadly, for their victims, Clueless Emperors predictably travel this harmful path. All too often, they behave as though the only way to be right is to stick with their original viewpoints. Those viewpoints evolve into agendas over time, and Clueless Emperors are well-known to forcefully defend their agendas to the point that anyone who questions or challenges them feels the pressure to fold. In the Emperors' minds, to even consider alternate perspectives means they were wrong, which their need-to-be-right attitudes won't allow them to do. This driving force may have contributed to the *Challenger* disaster.

We all enjoy the dopamine high of being right—it's human nature, brain chemistry at its luxurious best. But even though *liking to be right* is a common and relatively benign human trait, it's important to know that in certain circumstances some people will take this to the extreme of *needing to be right*. When this happens, meaningful information exchange comes to a screeching halt and communication can turn ugly. The need-to-be-right mindset takes hold when unaware people cling to their values and beliefs, despite new information that might have altered their thinking, if they were sufficiently skilled to be open-minded or cared enough about others to get over themselves.

Need-to-be-right behavior comes across as self-righteous. People in this frame of mind often require a major hit to their power base, self-esteem, or wallet before they wake up, if they ever wake up at all. But a jarring event of some kind is often required, because a *need* to be right is usually subconscious, outside a person's awareness, and linked to a lack of self-esteem.

How do we differentiate between *liking to be right* and *needing to be right?* People who *like to be right* certainly enjoy having the "answer"—most of us enjoy such moments—but at the same time, they're able to listen to perspectives different from their own and maintain a calm demeanor. They can easily carry on conversations and discussions with people who see things differently from the way they themselves see the issues. This skill comes in handy when there are problems to solve and easy solutions aren't apparent.

People who *need to be right* behave differently and are easy to spot. They don't listen. They look tense, they interrupt, they raise their volume, they use coarse or abusive language, point fingers, blame others, and do most of the talking. If they happen to have situation or position power during these emotional blackout periods, the people they intimidate become afraid, frustrated, or angry and communication breaks down. When there are problems to solve in these situations—nothing happens. There are no successful outcomes.

The near collapse of the American automobile industry is a good example of a group of Clueless Emperors listening only to themselves and ignoring anyone who disagreed with them. Their need-to-be-right mentality was rooted in their stubborn desire to avoid being wrong about supporting product lines that were no longer profitable and becoming less so each year. These executives didn't seem to understand that ignoring consumer market data contrary to the strategy they were advancing, and sticking with ineffective plans of their own, they achieved nothing more than making a bad situation worse. Stubbornness is a weapon of choice for most Clueless Emperors. They use their power to avoid what they perceive to be the "shame" of being wrong and give little thought to adjusting to a changing environment. Shareholders be damned.

What comes to mind when you hear the word *stubborn*? This word expresses an opinion, not a behavior, and we're likely to use it to describe someone we don't agree with, or who doesn't agree with us because of the negative connotation. The same behavior might be viewed quite differently when we see it in someone with whom we agree. The words we choose are often influenced by our emotions. For example, I've encountered Clueless Emperors who consider their own "stubbornness" to be a charming personality trait, while they view other people displaying the very same behavior as pigheaded.

The predicament with perception-based language is that it plays a big role in how people communicate—every day. However, if we know that words sometimes mean different things to different people, we also know that subjective opinions may need to be clarified from time to time. For our purposes, let's clarify, and assume the word *stubborn* is perceived by a majority of people to have a negative connotation. *Stubborn* implies unyielding or persistent, and usually not in a good way. *Willful obstinacy* probably comes close to what most people mean when they use the word *stubborn*. Conversely, when we think someone is being persistent for a positive purpose, the perception-based word *determined* might be used instead.

It's likely that "she's being stubborn" is the opinionated label we pin on someone just because her ideas challenge our thinking. We need to make her appear bad and wrong so we can be good and right. She may very well label us in the same way. The Scottish poet Robert Burns (1759–1796) showed insight when he wrote what a gift it would be to see ourselves as others see us (*Ode to a Louse, verse 8*). That gift is readily available, and good things happen when we're open to feedback and the feedback is effectively delivered. If only one of these two occurs, a positive result is less certain but still possible. If neither occurs, the chances of anything good happening are slim indeed.

Even though we can't legislate candid, open communication, our own skillfully delivered feedback often encourages others to do the same. When we're able to persuade Clueless Emperors to acknowledge the possibility of another approach, we allow them to save face—a precursor of change. As an example, imagine being on a road trip with a Clueless Emperor (whose power comes from owning the car and paying for the gas) who insists on taking a particular route you know, for a fact, is not the best one. How do you get him to change his mind? Coax him by saying you're not sure the selected route is the most efficient. Suggest that the two of you look at the map together—use plenty of charm in your tone. Make it seem as though he's doing you a big favor to check it out, and congratulate him when he finds the better route. If this behavior modification technique feels disingenuous, just remember it's not your car, not your gas money. At the same time, you would like to get your needs met.

The diplomatic approach will be far more effective than berating the Clueless Emperor, grabbing the map yourself, and pointing out the better route. A need-to-be-right person would do it that way. The goal with Clueless Emperors is to overcome their selfish thinking and improve decision making without acrimony. One-upmanship doesn't work well with anyone, but try it with a Clueless Emperor for a memory you won't soon forget.

When people hold fast to agendas that make no sense, they seldom realize what they're doing. Otherwise, why would they do it? A deeply embedded and stubborn need to be right blocks their attentiveness to the facts at hand. They single-mindedly focus on a selfish outcome, because they don't know any other way. When we label others as stubborn, we imply they know what they're doing, and the selfish behavior is deliberate. Closed minds are usually habitual and involuntary.

The emperor in Andersen's fairy tale (Appendix A) starts out in this mode. He is self-absorbed and blocks out reality to protect his fragile ego. It's only after the parade is well under way that the light bulb in his brain begins to glow, and he's finally able to admit, although only to himself, that the swindlers got the best of him. But the iron grip of his need to be right drives him to carry on with the parade anyway, even when he gets it that he's walking through town in his underwear. If he had stopped the parade, it would have indicated he had never seen the fabric in the first place. This just wasn't an acknowledgment he was willing to make. The emperor's behavior is a classic example of someone who needs to be right—no matter what.

How many people stand by their original positions, even after they realize their initial thinking was incorrect? Human nature taken to this extreme does not serve us well. Most people don't wake up in the morning with the explicit goal of being stubborn in everything they do that day. Some people may be stubborn on purpose (therefore not entirely clueless), but most of us are not so calculating. Has anyone ever called you stubborn? If so, you probably weren't conscious of your behavior at the time. You may even have felt unjustly accused by the label.

So how do we *not* leap to making a judgment that some so-and-so is stubborn? One way is to look in the mirror and assume *you* will be viewed as stubborn by someone who thinks you're not listening. Human nature suggests we're more generous when self-evaluating than when we evaluate others. This is especially true for people who staunchly defend their agendas and refuse to acknowledge other people's ideas. Let your biased and gentle self-evaluation tendency give way to a more objective view by putting yourself in someone else's shoes. Asking questions and listening to what people have to say is a good approach in such circumstances. When we focus on openness, even when it's uncomfortable to do so, our brains are better able to absorb information and judge less harshly.

A good understanding of the difference between *enjoying* being right (a common human tendency) and *needing* to be right (a pathological condition) provides vital insight. As a reminder, most people share a common impulsive desire to have the "answer," no matter what the question is. The liking-to-be-right mentality is deeply embedded in the minds of most decent, well-meaning citizens, so having this inclination doesn't make us bad; it merely shows we're human. After all, nobody *enjoys* being wrong.

Let's say two people are in conflict and unable to reach agreement when it's necessary to do so. Each of them might label the other as "stubborn." By sticking to their respective agendas, no matter what new information comes to light contradicting their positions, they remain deadlocked. Which one is correct? Or is each of them partly correct? Is there someone not even in the conversation who has better information? How should the parties reach a positive conclusion? Or worse, are *both* people completely ignorant of being wrong? Imagine what happens when opposing, incorrect viewpoints on important matters evolve into opposing agendas. This occurs in a broad spectrum of venues: from governments and large organizations, all the way to small volunteer groups and families. Closed minds open the door to disappointment and failure.

If we remain unaware of this human dynamic, we lose the opportunity to reach the best possible outcome. We dedicate energy toward advancing our agendas instead of seeking the information to understand the facts, solve problems, fix what's broken, or resolve conflicts. Historical evidence has shown over and over again that people with loads of power are especially reluctant to relinquish it. It's highly probable you'll interact, at least occasionally, with people who *need* to be right.

People with an *undying need* to be right are especially toxic. Steering clear of these people is a wise move, but sometimes they cannot be ignored, or will not go away. If they are work colleagues, family members, or people we live with, dodging them may not even be a choice. Feeling aggravated by the behavior of such a person often builds resentment, which in turn creates stress. As Larry Winget says in his book *Shut Up, Stop Whining & Get a Life* (Wiley, 2011, revised ed.), "stress occurs when we know the right thing to do, and we don't do it." I would add that skillful confrontation, over time, encourages people to do the right thing because results improve with this approach to communication.

The antidote to the need-to-be-right character flaw in oneself is to develop the ability to feel perfectly comfortable being wrong. Feeling comfortable with the *possibility* of being wrong is good, too. When this kind of thinking is the default mode, progress is more likely when a disagreement develops. But for most people, the need to *defend* is the default mode, so making this change is where the work begins. However strong it may be, banishing any need-to-be-right tendency from the brain, if there is one in residence, is crucial. But how can a brain be conditioned to resist this impulse?

The exercise I recommend consists of *privately questioning every statement you make for a period of time.* In other words, the goal of this exercise is to improve your ability to think before you speak, and make it a habit. With practice, you can develop a new attitude in short order, but you have to engage in rigorous practice. Trying this exercise every now and again will not achieve the desired outcome, because old habits aren't broken easily. Your practice must be consistent and relentless. Silently questioning every declarative statement begins to create an appropriate lack of certainty from time to time. The next step is to acknowledge that lack of certainty *out loud.* You could say something like, "I might be wrong about this," or "I'm not sure about that." If you know you're wrong, be forthright and say, "Well, I sure was wrong about (*fill in the blank*)!"

This won't be an easy mission for the need-to-be-right crowd, but the payoff is significant. As an aside, if you've developed a need-to-be-right attitude, you will astonish your friends, family members, and work colleagues with this new behavior. Be prepared for them to ask what wonderful new drug you're taking.

If you feel awkward in the early stages of this exercise, take comfort that it's a natural result of breaking a bad habit and forcing change. The specific words used to acknowledge being uncertain, or wrong, are not important. It's the "saying it out loud" part that makes the difference, even if there is noticeable stuttering the first few times. The success that comes with expunging the need to be right is exhilarating. You'll have a lifelong skill that will improve interactions with others and strengthen relationships.

This exercise may seem "too simple a cure" for the malady of *needing to be right,* but forced changes in behavior are known to encourage new ways of thinking. Letting go of a need-to-be-right attitude has benefits in a variety of situations. Two people who have relatively equal power, both of whom have stakes in the sand, don't get anywhere. They cancel each other out until one of them is willing to show vulnerability and break the logjam. On the other hand, when a Clueless Emperor is in the mix, anyone opposing him or her will likely lose. Should this happen to you, pull *your* stake out of the sand and start a real conversation. *Part III: Learning the Skills* provides details of the effective tactics to make that happen.

The ability to acknowledge being wrong has a double advantage: it not only prevents us from behaving like Clueless Emperors, but it's also an effective strategy for overcoming an Emperor. When we don't dig in our heels, conflicts are easily avoided. An I'm-not-sure-about-this attitude will disarm Clueless Emperors because there is nothing for them to fight, which allows an opposer to nudge them along to consider other options.

When people verbally acknowledge a lack of certainty, they can re-train their brains within days. But consistent practice can't be overemphasized—take a break, and bad old habits will return in no time. Common human defensiveness will disintegrate with the confidence built from this exercise. When the automatic need to defend disappears, the skill has been mastered. Any future need to defend will be a conscious and wise choice. Acknowledging we might be wrong about something creates opportunities for discussion. Try it, and see how well it works.

Showing vulnerability also provides a role model that encourages others to listen better and be more open to changing their own ways of thinking. When we question our beliefs and acknowledge mistakes, we communicate a sense of curiosity. People appreciate this. It allows them to have their own skin in the game. When we admit to not being sure about something, those with staunch opinions often drop their guard. Ironically, this occurs because we're capitalizing on *their* need to be right, and they begin to feel awkward trying to fight with someone who won't fight back.

The paradox is people inherently trust others more, not less, when they believe an admission of wrongdoing is genuine. Many famous people understood this human dynamic and have made public apologies over the years. I'm sure you can think of a few. Sometimes the authenticity of these apologies is questioned by the public, but rest assured, the apologizers' handlers knew this tactic has historically paid dividends if gaining public trust or approval is the goal.

It's helpful to know that showing vulnerability is often a way to gain sympathy, understanding, and forgiveness. Most people enjoy being in a position to forgive, so an apology is often an effective way to correct a mistake and rebuild trust. On the other hand, most people also have eagle eyes for insincerity, so make sure any apology you make is genuine, and that there is no intent to manipulate people's emotions.

Chapter 9 Main Points
The Harmful Agendas of Clueless Emperors

- Stubbornness is not a behavior. It's a perception.
- Liking-to-be-right is a common human frailty. Needing-to-be-right is a bigger problem that often causes conflict—know the difference and get an attitude adjustment if necessary.
- Maintaining one's position in the face of contrary data usually stems from a need-to-be-right mentality.
- If people don't effectively deal with the aggravation in their lives, resentment can build over time.
- Acknowledging a mistake or a lack of certainty is a skill that pays dividends.
- Assume that perception-based words may have different meanings for different people.

"It's odd—my self-confidence improves whenever I acknowledge I'm wrong."
—A Recovering Clueless Emperor

CHAPTER 10

When Power and Harmful Agendas Coincide

"I believe there are more instances of the abridgement of the freedom of the people by gradual and silent encroachments of those in power than by violent and sudden usurpations."
—James Madison

We've learned about the nature and characteristics of power, and how the need-to-be-right mindset encourages harmful agendas. What can we expect when these two forces coincide? When this happens, be assured the Clueless Emperors at the scene are ready, willing, and able to go cruising for prey and overtake anyone who appears vulnerable. It's important to understand the dynamics of what goes down when the unskilled version of you is accosted by a Clueless Emperor with a harmful agenda. Understanding how Clueless Emperors take control paves the way for more skillful negotiations with them. That's why there aren't any solutions in this chapter—on purpose. What you'll learn here is how to recognize the signs of an oncoming ambush.

Before we look at what materializes when power and harmful agendas coincide, it's important to be reminded that power and positive agendas also exist. Knowing the difference is essential when disagreements begin to emerge. Anyone who responds in a hostile or immature way to a positive agenda is behaving irresponsibly—this is Junior Clueless Emperor conduct. It's also helpful to know when one's own agenda is foolish or selfish. For our purposes here, let's assume your inner Clueless Emperor is under control, your facts are straight, and your agenda has a positive objective. This vantage point makes it easier to evaluate competing agendas. It's especially important to do this effectively with Clueless Emperors, because in these situations, right and wrong are commonly at stake.

However great our intentions or brilliant our thinking, when we're challenged by Clueless Emperors, any lack of good form on our part will play a significant role in how things turn out for us. As an example, if we talk too much, or too little, we undermine our credibility. If our form makes us appear meek on one end of the scale to arrogant on the other, whatever content we have to offer gets lost, and the opportunity to persuade goes right along with it. When influence really matters—let's say a family member is making bad choices and needs guidance, or an ill-informed boss is behaving like a child and needs feedback—wouldn't it be great to make a positive difference in situations like these? When the stakes in a conflict are high, and we fail to persuade Clueless Emperors to re-evaluate their positions and consider options, we also fail those who depend on us most.

Don't think that minimal power differences among people—where no one has enough authority to outrank the others—makes problem-solving easier. This just presents a potentially different kind of problem, especially when sufficient behavioral skills are in short supply. Very little if anything gets done. People just get mired in different kinds of messes. While it might be a relief to know there isn't a Clueless Emperor around, productivity comes to a standstill, nonetheless.

Let's look at an example where neither party has position power, or even apparent situation power, and individual agendas are in conflict: Brian and Renee are peers at the

WeCanDoIt Company. They have been working together on a big sale to a potential new client, WeNeedHelp Inc., where their point of contact, Anna, is making the buying decision. Both Brian and Renee think they know best how to interact with her, but their approaches differ. Brian says they need to take a soft-sell approach (based on *his* reading of her buying signals), providing abundant information about their product and allowing time for questions. Renee, on the other hand, thinks they need to strongly encourage Anna to decide soon (based on *her* reading of Anna's buying signals). Let's listen in on a conversation between Brian and Renee the day before a scheduled meeting with Anna.

Renee: "I really think Anna is ready to make a decision when we meet with her tomorrow."

Brian: "I hope you're not going to put any pressure on her—it would be a colossal mistake. So far, she's only asked for additional information. What we need to do is slow down and not push before she's ready. I don't want to lose this sale."

Renee: "Hey—last time I checked, my sales record is better than yours."

Brian: "That's not true, and you know it. You're trying to get out of finding all the information she wants."

Renee: "Look, I know what I'm doing here. What you're suggesting is a total waste of time, and I'm not going along with it. Just sit back tomorrow and watch the master at work."

Brian: "I won't agree to strong-arm her, so you better back off this approach, or you'll be embarrassed tomorrow—I'll make sure of it."

Renee: "Hey buddy, hold your horses. No need to get crazy over this thing."

What if the real problem between Brian and Renee is nothing more than each of them has a subconscious need to be right? Because they're unaware of this need, they argue their individual agendas instead of working with the facts and listening to each other's perspectives. And each of them sees the other as stubborn. Yes, they're both behaving like Junior Clueless Emperors, but neither of them has that awareness, nor the status to pull rank. They're deploying the personal power they have and canceling each other out. If Brian and Renee could watch a video of their conversation, they would probably feel embarrassed. Of course, it seldom happens that people have the option to see an instant replay of their behavior, so other tactics are required.

Imagine what would happen if *either* Brian or Renee was willing to let go of the need to be right. What if one of them had the skill to shift the focus of their disagreement to what is best for their customer? Now imagine the possibilities if *both* Brian and Renee had that ability. Their conversation would sound very different: the information Anna has given them, the details of the company's business objectives and an intelligent analysis of what they know is what we would hear. Their interaction, as it stands, shows that even power equity doesn't prevent controversy when there is a clash of agendas. If anything, it leads to a stalemate and no resolution of any kind—no one has enough authority to make a decision, for good or ill. Competing agendas, combined with a lack of good form, are enough to delay, or even prevent, a positive outcome.

So what happens when we add *power inequity* to the mix? Let's look at some examples of power differences between people with competing agendas. In each case, the Clueless Emperor has an incorrect or inappropriate agenda and, by definition, also enjoys the power advantage.

- Jeff purchased a case of wine at the local wine shop. The wine in the first two bottles he opened had turned sour, so he thinks there's a good possibility all the bottles have gone bad. He decides to return the whole case, but can't find the receipt. When he takes the case back to the store, customer representative Barbara—in Clueless Emperor mode—says in a bored-to-death drawl, "That's too bad. Store policy requires a receipt to make a return. You should try to find it." (*Barbara has situation power.*) If Barbara were to hide behind store policy, just because she can, and Jeff isn't persuasive enough to encourage her to adopt a customer focus, he might be stuck with a case of spoiled wine.
- One of the poorest performing students in teacher Joan's class is Sandra, the daughter of Ken, a notoriously arrogant school board member (*position power*). Joan wants to help Sandra improve her grades without incurring the father's indignation, but she also doesn't want to give Sandra a higher grade than she's earned just to keep Ken off her back.
- Anthony, who reports to manager Krista, was hired based on his father's connections to executives in the company. The father is a politician with a self-righteous, need-to-be-right reputation (*position power*). Anthony is not performing well in his job, and so far has resisted Krista's coaching. Krista wants to help him without putting her own job at risk. She further realizes that choosing to ignore the problem with him could also jeopardize her credibility—his poor performance would reflect badly on the department. Krista knows people at work are watching how she handles the Anthony problem. If she does nothing, she may be perceived as a manager who

avoids conflict or plays favorites. Krista feels that she doesn't have any good options to solve her problem.

- Amy has a chronic medical condition and has been seeing a highly regarded specialist for several years. She trusts his technical competence, but his bedside manner leaves something to be desired. Unfortunately, she regularly sits in the waiting room at least one hour for each appointment, and no one has ever acknowledged the consistent delays, let alone apologized. (*The doctor and his staff have situation power.*) She's grown weary of these predictably long waits, but she worries the doctor may treat her unfavorably if she speaks up about her frustration, and her wait time could become even longer.

- Manager Paula (*position power*) regularly takes credit for her employees' work. They want to receive proper acknowledgment for their accomplishments, but they keep these thoughts to themselves—they fear Paula may retaliate if they raise the issue with her.

- Sally has had a long-term friendship with Larry, the nice guy who cuts her hair—they've developed a bond over the years that is important to her. Sally has asked Larry several times for ideas to change her hairstyle, but he subtly ignores her requests and continues to cut her hair the same way at every appointment. (*Larry's possession of the scissors gives him situation power.*) Sally is ready to give up and try a new stylist, but she fears she will hurt Larry's feelings, and that he will no longer want to be her friend.

- Manager David (*position power*) asks Alison, his subordinate, to collect some information and generate marketing ideas for an important new product their company is introducing. Alison spends several hours on the assignment and is eager to meet with her boss. At their meeting, David sits stone-faced during her entire presentation, and then asks rhetorically, "Is that it?" When Alison nods, he proceeds to belittle her ideas and tells her to start over with something fresher and more innovative, then abruptly turns around in his chair to work at his computer.

In each of these examples, a person with power has a negative agenda to control the outcome of a conflict involving someone with less power. These short vignettes don't reveal motives, but it's important to remember that some Clueless Emperors pull rank for no other reason than to prove they can. Their autopilot is usually switched to the "compete" mode, and just like a shark, some of them can smell blood a mile away. There isn't necessarily a deep meaning at play when a Clueless Emperor takes advantage of power. Good form is the best ally in these situations.

Important information to remember: when either power inequities or agenda differences stand alone, they pose fewer communication hazards than when the two are combined. The following bullets provide definitions of the players:

- **Clued-In people** consistently acknowledge the ideas and viewpoints of others. Whatever power they have is used appropriately. They're easy to get along with and pose no threat.
- **Clueless people** stubbornly maintain their positions. They can be quite annoying, but pose no threat, because they lack sufficient power. When their behavior gets irritating enough, people can walk away and ignore them without fear of reprisal, and this is often what happens.
- **Clueless Emperors** misuse their power while promoting a foolish or selfish agenda, and consequently pose a

threat. Having the right skills to overcome these people is vital if a positive outcome is desired.

Chapter 10 Main Points
When Power and Harmful Agendas Coincide

- Agendas can have positive or negative purposes.
- Opposing agendas create conflict when both parties need to be right.
- The combination of power and harmful agendas poses serious communication challenges.
- There isn't any room to maneuver when conflict develops between parties with power equity. They cancel each other out and nothing happens.
- Don't let a positive agenda die needlessly—develop the skills to keep it alive.

"I used to push people around. Now I persuade them instead."
—A Recovering Clueless Emperor

Using Emotion Effectively

"Intellect is to emotion as our clothes are to our bodies; we could not very well have civilized life without clothes, but we would be in a poor way if we had only clothes without bodies."
—Alfred North Whitehead

The familiar adage *It isn't what you say, it's how you say it* has been quoted as accepted wisdom for a long time. Even though people often recognize the inherent truth in this cliché, it's ironic that most of us don't acknowledge its validity by following through with our behavior. It bears repeating that people tend to spend far more time developing the content of what they want to communicate than developing the form they'll use to deliver that content. We already know this is not productive. *How* a message is delivered is essential. Why? Because the *how* connects our content to the *emotions* of our audience. All the physical skills required to make that happen are coming up in *Part III: Learning the Skills*, but the information in those chapters presumes you have the emotional element in hand. That's what this chapter is all about.

Some people resist the idea that emotion plays a role in communication, but if this were true, we would all talk like robots with no voice inflection or changes in volume. Perhaps we'd sound like Mr. Spock. Our writing wouldn't need any punctuation or words that describe emotions, and our bodies wouldn't move a muscle when we talked.

Emotion, for good or ill, is embedded in all communication. Even though some of us are uncomfortable acknowledging the power of emotion, our discomfort doesn't make it disappear. There's no question—learning how to skillfully weave emotion into what we say and write provides advantages. It's essential when we have disagreements with Clueless Emperors, because they specialize in bypassing emotion to block progress. Stifling feelings translates to colluding with them—don't help Clueless Emperors by doing their job for them.

How many times have you suffered through a talk or presentation that may have had good content, but was delivered in such mind-numbing style you would have rather watched paint dry than listen to it? If a speaker is boring, even when listeners force themselves to pay attention, no one is persuaded. And the boredom factor doesn't just apply to formal presentations. How many times have you tuned out while a friend rambled on in a monotone about something or other? Tuning out usually has more to do with *how* the message is delivered than with *what* is said.

On the opposite end of that scale, think about comedians who win over an audience without much content at all—their delivery style compels us to listen. But you don't need to be a comedian to get people to pay attention. If your delivery method persuasively supports the message, people will listen and take note of what you have to say. It's just not acceptable to hold back emotion and come across as boring when there are so many ways to be interesting and engaging.

The people on the receiving end of a boring message rarely give feedback about their pain, so speakers are usually clueless about their dreary delivery. Most "listeners" sit and daydream, counting the minutes until the talking finally stops, so they can be relieved of their duty: sitting quietly while bored to tears. Now turn that situation around. Do you want people to tune you out and suffer through what you have to say?

Wouldn't it be better to inspire them to want more? Powerful emotion motivates people to act; emotionless communication motivates people to yawn. One of the keys to sustaining the interest of listeners is the ability to productively combine the emotional element of a message with content. But first, it's necessary to be persuaded of the merit to do so. Read on.

In relationships with friends and family, cautionary messages to suppress emotion are common. Perhaps you've been warned to keep emotions in check. This is typically more often true for males in our culture, but it also gets applied to females. Through socialization, we learn "boys don't cry" and "girls should be sugar and spice and everything nice." Warnings to set our emotions aside are heard across a broad range of settings from playgrounds, schools, and homes—to workplaces, executive suites, and boardrooms. But these warnings make no sense: zipped up leads to locked up and repressed emotion just goes underground.

On the other end of the emotional spectrum is the inability to manage emotion altogether. As an example, losing one's temper is often a result of an accumulation of locked-up emotions that reaches a tipping point at a particular moment. Think of a circumstance when you've become aggravated over something small and realized, after the fact, that your real frustration was about something else entirely. Even though most of us understand this driving force, we continue to perpetuate the myth that emotion should be removed from the communication equation.

However diligently we may struggle, emotions are going to show up in our behavior, one way or another. Most people can't conceal emotion with any consistency, so it's unrealistic to try. When feelings eventually surface, despite best efforts to push them down or deny them, they sometimes rise up in very unproductive ways. Road rage is an extreme example. Most people don't explode over a bad driver who cuts them off. They are exploding over events that occurred before that bad driver ever showed up. Why not learn to manage emotion rather than let it fester and eventually materialize at the wrong time, with the wrong person, in a punishing way? Emotional hijackings never serve any useful purpose.

How many meetings, functions, or family affairs have you attended where there is obvious tension no one is brave enough to address? The pent-up feelings of the participants come out later, sometimes in the form of destructive backbiting. How many family relationships are harmed in these situations? Most of us have heard of family feuds where relatives haven't spoken to each other for years because of some perceived injustice, the specifics of which no one even recalls. And sometimes that ill will gets passed down to the next generation of family members who continue to carry the baggage, even though they may have had nothing to do with the grudges in question.

In business situations, how often is productivity slowed down or stalled completely when emotions in disguise take over? Phrases such as "elephant in the room" and "the 800-pound gorilla" have been invented to describe this phenomenon. What can make a difference? Emotional intelligence is indispensable.

I am not, of course, advocating inappropriate displays of emotion. High drama is unproductive. What I am advocating is *emotional control*. Awareness of the emotional potential in a situation and being able to properly channel it provides benefits. How can emotions be effectively controlled? Like anything else, when we don't know how to do something, it's just a matter of learning how to do it.

One great way to learn is to verbalize feelings, which tends to prevent behaviorally *acting out* feelings. As an example, discuss frustrations and concerns directly with the person involved, and it will likely prevent inappropriate behavior down the road. If you don't feel confident doing this, find a skilled coach and ask for advice. For instance, let's say you're upset with a friend—and emotions are raw—so you want advice before talking with him. Just remember that talking to everyone *except* the person is called gossiping—which won't solve the problem. I want to emphasize that direct communication is usually best, and it's also true these kinds of conversations need to be handled skillfully. Upcoming chapters provide guidance on how to do that. The first important step is to understand that emotions left on a lit burner will eventually boil over and burn, so they must be managed in a productive way.

Using vocal inflection is another excellent tactic for linking content to emotion. A tone of voice that accurately reflects how you feel (do you say you're excited, but sound bored to death? or say you're fine, but sound furious?) will enhance the *how* of a message. Do you ever have to guess how people are feeling? What is the effect on communication if you guess wrong? Emotions inwardly acknowledged and outwardly expressed don't require guesswork. Communication is effective and misunderstandings can be cleared up on the spot.

A third way to communicate emotion is to say it explicitly out loud. Here are some examples—the felt emotion is given in boldface:

"I'm **excited** about this work project."
"I'm **worried** that we'll be late."
"I'm **happy** about your promotion."
"I'm **sad** about what happened to you."
"I'm **grateful** for your help."
"I'm **surprised** you haven't finished the project as you promised."

Verbalizing words that describe your emotional state helps listeners better understand the content you wish to convey. When you want to know someone else's emotional state, check in with questions (*Are you concerned about that choice?*) or observations (*You seem concerned about that choice.*) to get information. The common and somewhat mechanical question, "How are you?" followed by the perfunctory answer, "Fine," doesn't count; this phrase is usually expressed as a greeting, not a real question. If you really want to know, ask specific questions to get information that might otherwise have gone unspoken.

Ask people about their emotional state to show that you care. It's surprising that simply asking people how they're doing (gracefully, of course), and truly wanting to know, is a behavior that's rarely used. Pay attention, and you'll see for yourself. Begin using this skill to experience the rewards—it builds relationships and creates trust when done authentically.

These two quotations are favorites of mine that nicely sum up the influence that emotion has on communication, and why we shouldn't ignore it:

- *"Let's not forget that the little emotions are the great captains of our lives and we obey them without realizing it."* —Vincent Van Gogh
- *"Any emotion, if it is sincere, is involuntary."* —Mark Twain

Chapter 11 Main Points
Using Emotion Effectively

- Emotion is embedded in our daily communication. We can't eliminate it.
- Negative emotions left to simmer will eventually boil over and burn.
- Describing how you're feeling can enhance communication.
- Checking in to see how people feel is a great way to deepen mutual understanding and build trust.

"I feel like the Tin Man after he got a heart."
—A Recovering Clueless Emperor

The Awareness Advantage

"If ignorant both of your enemy and yourself,
you are certain to be in peril."
—Sun Tzu

We know how Clueless Emperors conduct themselves: they use their power in foolish or selfish ways for personal gain. We also know their behavior often prevents civilized citizens from making a contribution or achieving a goal. What all Clueless Emperors have in common is a lack of sufficient awareness. This deficiency acts like a sedative in their bodies, keeping them in their clueless state. The information in this chapter explores how sharpening awareness can help you overcome Clueless Emperors as well as develop positive relationships with people who aren't Emperors.

Heightened awareness provides a considerable advantage for those who have it. Awareness, as it's used here, means consciously noticing behavior—and recognizing there is meaning associated with behavior. For our purposes, I'll discuss awareness from two vantage points:

1. Understanding your own actions—are you conscious of emotions, and do you understand why you do what you do? Or is autopilot your method of operation?
2. Understanding the actions of others—do you notice their behaviors, however subtle, or do you take people in at a superficial level?

At the end of this chapter, you will have answers to these questions and have techniques to raise awareness. The advice applies to *anyone* we spend time with, including family members, work colleagues, friends, and even social acquaintances or business contacts with whom we have brief interactions. With a solid level of awareness, people are able to:

1. Assess their current behaviors and decide which ones work and which need to change
2. Notice other people's behaviors
3. Evaluate the indirect feedback they receive from others
4. Differentiate between content and form
5. Determine how to effectively integrate content and form

Even though awareness is a mental acuity rather than a behavioral skill, the behavioral exercises in this chapter will help you develop awareness—of yourself and others. You will have the insight to specifically understand why so many people don't know how to consistently get along with others, develop relationships, and build trust to get things done. If you currently feel a connection to this clueless group, you need not remain among them any longer.

Self-awareness helps people make the transition from clueless to Clued-In. It's much easier, of course, to see the Clueless Emperor behavior in other people than in oneself: we cannot see ourselves, but we certainly do see the behavior of others. Even so, there is a way around this problem. If self-evaluation has not previously been a strength, it's never too late to start paying attention. As human beings, we unfortunately have boundless capacity to ignore information that contradicts our habits, values, and beliefs. Conversely, quality of life predictably improves with the awareness advantage, so it's worth the effort to develop this ability.

I'll share a personal example of a meeting I will never forget. Several years ago I was invited to coffee by a new acquaintance I'll call Gary. We had been introduced by mutual friends, and I was looking forward to socializing and getting to know him. What did our first meeting tell me? Gary was a non-stop talker. He dominated our conversation to the point that I finally stopped any attempts to interact. It would have been awkward for me to get up and leave, so I sat back, enjoyed my coffee, and pretended to listen. He was the Clueless Emperor at our table that day, with me as his captive audience. This gave him situation power.

I was impatient for him to notice my silence—I didn't utter a peep—but he apparently considered it an invitation to continue his monologue. My lack of participation finally seemed to have a slight effect—he didn't seem surprised when I interrupted, grabbing an opportunity as he was taking a breath, and said I needed to get home. But he surprised me on our way out of the coffeehouse with this question: "I talked too much, didn't I?" *He's been down this road before with others,* I thought to myself. *He's indicating he has at least some awareness of his behavior.* It was clear, though, that partial awareness had not been enough—he definitely needed to put pedal to the metal and finish the trip. So why did Gary dominate our conversation? He wasn't just *woefully* ignorant, which is somewhat explainable. He seemed to be *willfully* ignorant—no excuses acceptable.

My response to his question went something like, "Oh, I guess it seemed important for you to tell me about your interests." I didn't give a direct answer. I changed the subject instead and answered a question he hadn't asked, and not surprisingly, he didn't probe any further. On the surface it may seem I wasn't appropriately forthright, but my response was intended to prevent any bad feelings between us. The purpose of our get-together had been purely social. I had not met him prior to our coffee meeting, and now I had no reason to meet with him again. My only penance was to sit quietly in the coffeehouse on one occasion and wait him out, which I did out of respect for the mutual friends who had introduced us.

We can use this little story to examine how lack of awareness can sabotage even a just-getting-to-know-you relationship. It's also an example of how quickly situation power can materialize. Although this was just a social meeting, first impressions are especially important in business relationships. As an example, if Over-Talker-Gary had behaved that way in a job interview, he would have been seriously ignored.

Initially, Gary and I came together as peers with power equivalence. I wasn't expecting anything from him; nor did he expect anything from me. He quickly gained situation power, however, when I wanted to give up on our lopsided "conversation" and escape. We also had different agendas. He had some kind of need, perhaps subconscious, to control the interaction, and I had expected to participate in a conversation. His question about over-talking came too late to repair the problem he had created. Whether Gary was conscious of his behavior during the time we were together didn't matter. Whatever his intentions may have been, the outcome for me didn't change.

Please note that uncivilized behavior isn't usually excused because a person's intentions were good before "committing the crime." Actions matter more than intentions. The phrase "I didn't mean to *(fill in the blank)*" is a good one to eliminate from anyone's vocabulary when it's used as an excuse for inappropriate behavior.

Awareness is an essential ability required to overcome Clueless Emperors. I say essential because the behavior required to convey content can't be skillfully executed without it. As a reminder, awareness is a cognitive aptitude, so it can't be seen or heard when you have it, but it does influence our behavior. The popular cartoon figure that illustrates a glowing light bulb inside a person's head, implying knowledge or recognition, shows this ability very well. So, although awareness isn't a behavior, *being aware* is a crucial building block for learning the skills to overcome Clueless Emperors. As an example, Over-Talker-Gary will continue to exhibit Clueless Emperor tendencies until he gains full awareness of his non-stop chatter. Until the time I met him, partial awareness had not been enough to change his behavior. It seemed that I was just the last in a long line of people he had conversationally dominated based on his (rhetorical?) question about talking too much.

While awareness requires cognitive ability and mental health, average amounts of both are sufficient to achieve a respectable level of this ability—so most of us have the resources to improve in this area. How much intelligence and mental health are required? By reading this book, you're showing an interest in wanting to be a better communicator, which indicates you have the raw material to enhance your awareness. Some people, however, will never achieve awareness—a sad fact of life.

It's important to know the situations and people to avoid, and with whom and where you have the potential to succeed. Our decisions may not always be right, but the odds will improve if we collect relevant facts and make wise choices to cultivate relationships with people who show an interest in improving awareness and abandon people who don't. Take advantage of your options when you're on the receiving end of Clueless Emperor Behavior. Your job is not to save the world. At the same time, of course, you still need to develop the skills to be armed and prepared for conflict should you ever have occasion to save the world, or any small part of it.

Brain power and mental health are negatively affected by

physiological or psychological addictions such as drugs, alcohol, and gambling. These conditions substantively block awareness. I use these examples because most of us know someone with an addiction of some kind and have at least secondhand knowledge of how powerful addictions can be. Clinical interventions can help addiction sufferers gain awareness, but this book has a different goal—to improve mainstream awareness deficiency, not fix clinical problems.

Let's proceed with the assumption that your intelligence and mental health are solid, which means that awareness-raising potential is positive. Awareness of oneself makes it easier to notice the behavior of others, so I'll focus on self-awareness first. Paying attention to the feedback we receive is a great place to start this journey, but self-awareness is rarely gained through feedback from a single source.

People are more likely to become self-aware if they're given consistent, direct feedback from several sources. An argument could be made that effective feedback given just one time should be enough to register, and sometimes it is, but most human beings are innately too defensive to act on feedback they've received only once. More often, people need to hear the same message numerous times from different sources before it finally soaks in, and even then, it sometimes doesn't make a difference. The sooner we let down our guard, the sooner we understand the messages being sent.

A second way to achieve self-awareness is to notice indirect feedback. This method is less efficient, because indirect feedback is … well, less direct. Back for a moment to the story about Over-Talker-Gary: my self-imposed silence is an example of indirect feedback. When he asked whether he had talked too much, Gary was indicating prior knowledge of his behavior, but also that it hadn't yet motivated him to change. My silence seemed to slightly register on his personal Richter scale, so perhaps it caused a new fissure in his denial. Every little bit can help—there is usually a tipping point somewhere. Gary's ignorance is not unusual in this regard, and he personifies why developing the awareness advantage is so worthwhile.

People who pay attention to indirect feedback will be more aware of how they're perceived. Unfortunately, few people do this effectively—a shame, because it's such a simple task. Some people have to hit bottom before they comprehend potential improvement areas. I hope this book keeps you safe from needing that kind of wake-up call.

The human characteristic of liking-to-be-right and having answers for any and all questions also causes us to miss feedback signals. Making excuses for bad decisions is the lifeblood of the unaware. When people are in this frame of mind, they don't pick up on the indirect feedback that may contradict their thinking. It's too subtle to penetrate their self-protection armor, which makes them indifferent to any change messages that might come their way. But many of us ignore even the clear and direct signals people send. We want to be right, so we feel we must defend the things we've always believed, and the way we've always done things. That's when our inner shark is out of its cage and cruising freely, looking for some fun.

An important step toward achieving heightened self-awareness is to get comfortable with change. This feeling is a natural result of questioning the familiar habits and motives that have been reassuring in the past and consciously evaluating whether they're serving us well, or not. It's easier to change habits when we can acknowledge that prior choices may not have been the best ones, and when the satisfaction previously gained from those choices begins to fade. Comfort with change starts to happen when we can say to ourselves: *No big deal—I made a bad choice. I can change and move forward.* We no longer need to defend what we *used* to do because we're consciously and willingly making a different choice *now*. This mental transition occurs when the brain gets trained to think less defensively.

An exercise to create a new brain pathway that doesn't automatically go on the defensive: *consciously pay close attention to how you respond to other people's agendas when they differ from yours*. This is an exercise to train your brain to accept new information without fighting it—don't worry, you won't have to do this forever. Our brains quickly adapt when we're motivated to improve.

It's surprising how often people intensely defend their ideas or viewpoints in small but powerful ways each day, sometimes irrationally, for no other reason than habit. Examples are "Apple versus Microsoft" or "meat-eater versus vegetarian" arguments. Discussing the merits of opinions you're passionate about is fine, but unproductively fighting to defend your position is silly—yet people do this all the time. You'll see for yourself when you practice this exercise. Notice how difficult it is to change your position on any stance you've taken, no matter how inconsequential, even when it makes sense to do so.

As an example, several years ago I was asked to negotiate a truce between two coworkers who weren't cooperating with each other—we'll call them Kevin and Shellie. Their conflict escalated when Kevin publicly commented about Shellie spending too much time on personal business during work hours. In response, Shellie publicly protested that Kevin wasted plenty of time himself. She grumbled about his disgraceful non-use of technology. She hinted that cell phone communication and e-mail were foreign practices to him—and his sl-o-o-o-w hunt-and-peck typing method was pitiful to watch. Their squabble began to affect the productivity of their work groups. Although Kevin and Shellie each had valid insight into the other, neither of them was willing to acknowledge any personal shortcoming. They blamed each other while defending their own behaviors, and the company paying their salaries became the loser. Human resources was called in to help them achieve an understanding of how they each contributed to the problem and end their ridiculous conflict.

I acknowledge a negotiation like this can be delicate when Junior Clueless Emperors are involved. On the other hand, there is no reason people shouldn't be held accountable for having the skills to resolve these kinds of conflicts on their own. Should organizations be paying for this kind of referee service? Would companies pay employees who didn't know the technical requirements of their jobs? Yet poor form is often tolerated, even though it diminishes productivity and causes high cost overhead. Clueless Emperors provide a fair amount of job security for the human resources function.

These kinds of conflicts don't just occur between individuals. When people come together in organizational settings and collectively operate this way, the setbacks they cause can be significant. When products and services aren't modified to reflect new technologies and changing consumer demand, many enterprises go out of business because they didn't see the change coming.

As an example, it will be interesting to see how the United States food and restaurant industry adjusts to the escalating overweight and obesity statistics in our country. Consumer demand in this market is changing, and industry leaders that monitor, understand, and accept those changes will have to shift their products and services if they plan to survive. The food and beverage industry has generated lots of revenue by flipping high-fat burgers, putting potatoes in deep-fat fryers, and pouring sugar syrup into bottles—and many companies are still going strong with this business model. Adjustments are never easy when output is profitable, but evaluating market trends and planning for the future is required for sustainability. McDonald's, Applebee's, and Cheesecake Factory are examples of major restaurant chains keeping pace with the times. Their healthy menu additions indicate an awareness of a changing market.

Examples of companies in other industries where market trends went unheeded: why didn't Howard Johnson, Polaroid, A&P, or F.W. Woolworth executives adjust their strategies when consumer demand began to shift? Or even later when it became clear it was imperative to do so? Change is difficult, especially if there isn't pressure to act, so it's common for enterprises to roll along and maintain status quo, assuming customers won't ever want anything different. They defend current state when anything new comes along that challenges what they thought they knew for sure. Unfortunately for some, the pressure to change comes so quickly, in such a formidable dose, there simply isn't time to fix problems.

Whether a problem is big and complex or even small and simple, defensiveness is how human beings commonly respond to the pressure of change. *An idea of my own creation may not be the best idea ever*, we deep-down say to ourselves, *but by gosh, it's mine.* Yes, defensiveness is habit-forming, but it has to move out if awareness is going to move in.

If you want to gain control of your automatic defense mechanisms, practicing control will help. For instance, to personalize this, when you hear something disagreeable, *remain silent* for a few moments before you reply. There isn't a rule in the universe that says an immediate response on your part is required, so sit back and try to relax. Let's consider some simple examples of how gut reactions might play out in real life. Think about how you would respond in each situation:

- You and a friend go to a movie. On the way out of the theater, you're thinking the movie was one of the worst you've seen, and you're getting ready to say so, when your friend exclaims, "Wasn't that a great movie!"
- Your boss tells you to change some PowerPoint slides you spent hours creating and will be presenting yourself. You think the changes will make the slides less effective, and after all, it's not your boss who will be presenting them.
- Your sister insists you attend an informal family get-together that you have decided to skip in favor of badly needed sleep.
- Your spouse is adamant that the next family vacation should be working on projects at home. You spent the last two family vacations doing this. For next year's vacation, you want relaxation time away from home, preferably somewhere exotic.
- Your talented, intelligent child has brought home a less-than-stellar report card and doesn't seem remotely concerned about it.
- As you are driving down the freeway, your passenger makes a comment about tailgating.
- A colleague you were counting on for support is late for an important meeting and misses your agenda item. He blames traffic for his late arrival, when it's a given that traffic is a normal everyday problem and should have been accounted for.
- Another colleague you were counting on for support is late for the same important meeting and also misses your agenda item. She blames her late arrival on the alarm not going off, when it's a given that the alarm clock didn't develop a personality overnight and remain silent that morning on purpose.

A quick reaction in these examples might be to defend, blame, or argue, but these kinds of responses will probably lead to a negative conversation. Please don't think the only alternative is to be passive and surrender. Quite the contrary. *Stop and think.* Absorb what you've heard, evaluate the information, determine your preferred outcome, then wrap up your mini-analysis with a great delivery. The chapters on physical skills just ahead give recommendations for how to do this, but managing first-reaction defensiveness is the beginning step. The manner in which we respond to anything disagreeable has the potential to open the door to further conversation that might generate new ideas, or at the very least, keep the interaction alive.

An ineffective choice is to shut the door, not consider any alternatives, and maintain one's original position. Unfortunately, this is often what happens—and it's a Clueless Emperor specialty. Of course, every situation is different, but unique challenges aside, reducing defense mechanisms is the best friend of clear thinking. Our intelligence and delivery skill are then freed up to respond in a Clued-In manner when someone disagrees with us, disappoints us, makes an unexpected suggestion, or wants to do something we're initially not inclined to do.

Try this if you want to become more aware of your defense mechanisms: for the next couple of months, pay close attention to situations where some type of change is expected in your day-to-day activities. Life usually provides abundant opportunities to practice this exercise. Examples include things like needing to take a new route to work because of road construction (is this frustrating for you, or no big deal?), being asked to take a new project (is this worrisome, or exciting?), or maybe a last-minute request to chaperone your kid's school party (no problem, or big problem?).

Keep track of your spontaneous responses to change situations that come along, and you'll become sensitized to any innate and habitual defensiveness—a good thing to know, because a gut response isn't necessarily a reliable predictor of success. Is it common for you to stand by an original position when your autopilot is on? Be aware that most people prefer routines, even when the "familiar" isn't necessarily working in their best interests. That's how habits get developed and eventually become entrenched in day-to-day behavior. The goal of this exercise is to write the instruction manual for how your autopilot operates and learn how to control it.

As a supplement to this practice, challenge yourself to find ways to *agree* with ideas or change requests that initially feel contrary to your thinking. Disagreement and defensiveness are not allowed. Any suggestion that isn't compatible with what you believe or what you want to do is an opportunity to experiment. Pay attention (become aware), and you will find many, many opportunities to practice: how you drive, what you say, how much you talk, who you do business with, where you go, what you eat, when you arrive—are everyday examples.

Have a go at combining this developing-awareness exercise with the exercise in Chapter 9 where we discussed getting comfortable with being wrong. The two issues are related, and you may find synergy by practicing them at the same time. You might feel awkward in the early stages of practice—you'll be hyper-alert to anything different from a normal routine—but the feeling will be temporary.

Over the years, many people I've coached say they feel uncomfortable when they first try these exercises. Sometimes they even report not being able to think clearly (or at least what they had previously interpreted as clarity) when they start practicing. It's the brain's resistance to new ways of thinking and behavior, and explains why there are so many books, consultants, and therapists trying to help people cope with change. If you keep it simple and don't overcomplicate this exercise, you will respond less defensively without needing a therapist! Keep in mind that the autopilot in your brain can be friend or foe. Keeping the friend and managing the foe is where the work is. If your personal shark is acting up, maneuver him into shallow water and let him flop around until he's too exhausted to cause trouble.

The most compelling reason to go through the effort of increasing awareness is that without it, failure is inevitable. We won't recognize the Clueless Emperor behavior in ourselves, let alone in anyone else. The best friend of a bad habit is cluelessness, which is fueled by a lack of awareness. If we continue to do what we've always done, change won't happen. After all, it's just not possible to know what we haven't yet learned. In large organizational systems, when lives and economies are at stake, it's unforgivable to be clueless. The solution to this problem is to raise awareness through the prescribed exercises in this book and achieve Clued-In status.

Another good way to expand awareness is to ask trusted people for developmental feedback. Be specific with the request. Perhaps you need to become more aware of your tone of voice in conversations. Maybe you need to know whether you use conversational fillers—all those "uhs," and "ums," "likes," and "y' knows." Do you want to find out if you talk too much, or not enough? Chapters 14 and 15 will provide options for those who aren't currently Clued-In to the techniques required for good form.

A word of caution, however: please don't ask for feedback and act like a Clueless Emperor when you get it, even if the feedback isn't delivered well. Defensive reactions don't encourage people to supply information. Take a deep breath and remember that the feedback you receive is nothing more than information, and it belongs to you. It's your choice to act on it, or ignore it, if that makes the most sense. Not all feedback has value. If you ignore *all* the feedback you get, that's a different problem. A gracious, non-defensive reaction to feedback, no matter the quality, is the only effective response. Sometimes a simple and well-meaning "thank you" is all you need to say.

Before we leave this chapter, a word needs to be said about Clueless Emperors who don't see any logical need to raise awareness, because they have sufficient power to steamroll anyone who gets in their way. Practically speaking, it's understandable that those who have extraordinary position power don't see any advantage to improve awareness, or can't imagine they have anything to gain. If you fall into this category, listen up.

We can all name powerful people throughout history who have fallen off their pedestals. Richard Nixon is an iconic example. As analytically intelligent as he was, he lacked the self-awareness to see how his defensive and vengeful actions contributed to an inevitable downfall. Would the skill of awareness be useful if your pedestal wobbled? Wouldn't it be better if the pedestal never wobbled in the first place? It's true that Clueless Emperors sometimes escape appropriate comeuppance during their lifetime, but do you really want to take that chance? After all, maybe luck will prevail and you'll die first. To be fair, Ken Lay died shortly before he would have gone to prison for his significant role in the Enron scandal. Anything is possible, but wouldn't it be preferable to have better odds and be ahead of the curve?

Self-aware people have advantages and are far more likely to understand and learn from the ineffective behaviors of others. Their raised consciousness makes them less likely to get shark bites from Clueless Emperors. They're able to resist the Emperors' manipulative attempts because they know how to manage their own behavior. They also are able to observe from a distance—a great way to figure out what works and what doesn't, without the stress of learning through trial and error.

Chapter 12 Main Points
The Awareness Advantage

- By nature, human beings have boundless capacity to ignore what they don't want to know.
- Awareness helps people "know."
- Awareness is cognitive, not behavioral.
- It's easier to gain awareness of others' behaviors when you have self-awareness.
- We can improve self-awareness by focusing on how we react to other people.
- We can improve self-awareness by paying attention to how others react to us.
- We can improve self-awareness by getting feedback from people we trust.
- Clueless Emperors who take no action to improve their awareness are gambling they won't get caught. It's not worth the risk.

"I found comfort in my own skin once I achieved the awareness advantage."
—A Recovering Clueless Emperor

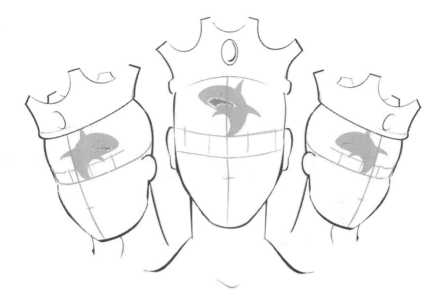

PART III
Learning the Skills

The Behavioral Menu

"Problems cannot be solved at the same level of
awareness that created them."
—Albert Einstein

Until now, the information in this book has been presenting evidence to convince and prepare you to get your form up to par with your content. Now is the time to meet that challenge. This chapter sets the stage for learning how to capture what's inside your head and convey it to the outside world in a persuasive and engaging way. You will learn how your voice and body can be impressive assets when Clueless Emperors are misbehaving and halting progress. The skills work with the Clued-In crowd as well, so you can expect to be a more effective communicator in general, once you've mastered them.

The advice here isn't intended to turn you into a movie star or stage performer; nor will you be asked to change your personality. What the skills *will* do is ensure that your thoughts get the best possible treatment before they depart the inner sanctum of your mind. We all want to express ideas effectively, but sometimes we just plain botch that objective. If you've ever wondered, after the fact, how you could have "said it better," the answers are right here.

The ideas inside our heads, of course, cannot be seen or heard. It's the source of our content, and absent an effective delivery vehicle, those ideas would be better off remaining inside our heads. Poor delivery of information, in any setting, is a waste of everybody's time, yours included. Clueless Emperors count on poor delivery of information—it's what they capitalize on to send unsophisticated challengers packing. How you communicate with them needs to come from a position of strength, which means that without good form, you're destined to fail.

The information in the next two chapters is straightforward and specific, sometimes brutally frank. If you feel yourself bristling at any of the advice, take note that the Clueless Emperor in your brain might be launching a shark attack, hoping that the hard work ahead can be avoided, even though continued cluelessness will be the result. Habits are powerful motivators to maintain current state, so resist the temptation to do nothing. The well-intentioned guidance ahead is for your thoughtful consideration—it's a personal decision whether or not to act on it.

Before we delve into specifics, I have a suggestion for how to calculate the effectiveness of the skills you'll be reading about in the chapters ahead. It's a guideline I call the 8-out-of-10 rule. This principle should bring peace of mind if the new skills don't work every time you use them. It may seem on the surface that people's reactions to what they see and hear can't be predicted, but remember this rule: although it's impossible to know how each and every person is going to interpret a specific behavior, we can predict how the majority will. For example, imagine someone out for a morning walk who sees someone approaching, so he smiles and says hello. Chances are the person passing by will smile and say hello back. Some people won't respond this way, but give or take, 8-out-of-10 people will.

In the same manner, the information in the next two chapters will be effective with 8-out-of-10 people, meaning there will be exceptions. The skills won't work with everyone all the time. They're intended as recommendations that will work with most people, most of the time. Keep this in mind as you digest the information. If you're thinking at any point, as an example, *This behavior will never work with Aunt Margaret,* you could be right; it might not. When this happens, go back and remember the rule.

I haven't scientifically researched the 8-out-of-10 rule— it's based on common sense and years of experience. Research is a dependable tool, but some things are intuitively logical. Smiles, sneers, shouts, whispers, laughter, frowns, and the hundreds of other behaviors people exhibit each day are decoded and similarly interpreted by the people who "receive" them. Not everyone will interpret a gesture or facial expression in the same way, but 8-out-of-10 people will. Movie directors and advertising copywriters understand this principle and take advantage of it. You can, too.

Most of us are not aware of how others perceive us. A universal shortage of developmental feedback and no practical way to get instant replays of our behavior make it tough to know how we come across to others. We have few if any clues about how we are seen and heard—unless we're famous personalities and followed around by paparazzi.

The information coming up will help you become more conscious of your current habits, and the recommendations given add up to a winning audible and visible presence. These skills last a lifetime, work just about everywhere with just about everyone, and will give the Clueless Emperors in your future some real competition.

The ability to differentiate between behaviors and perceptions provides a strong foundation for successfully executing the physical skills, and explains how our behaviors are interpreted by the people who observe and evaluate us. Keep this distinction in mind—it will prompt you to be precise and careful with form at all times and help with the execution of the physical skills. Review Chapter 7 if you need a refresher.

People with effective delivery skills are perceived more favorably than those who don't present themselves well—it's that simple. An iconic example of this is the first televised debate between John Kennedy and Richard Nixon in 1960. By all historical accounting, Kennedy won the presidency based on his behavioral skills in that debate. Kayla Webley described the event in an article for *Time* titled "How the Nixon-Kennedy Debate Changed the World" (September 23, 2010):

> "*What happened after the two candidates took the stage is a familiar tale. Nixon, pale and underweight from a recent hospitalization, appeared sickly and sweaty, while Kennedy appeared calm and confident. As the story goes, those who listened to the debate on the radio thought Nixon had won. But those listeners were in the minority. By 1960, 88% of American households had televisions— up from just 11% the decade before. The number of viewers who tuned in to the debate has been estimated as high as 74 million, by the Nielsen of the day,* Broadcast Magazine. *Those that watched the debate on TV thought Kennedy was the clear winner. Many say Kennedy won the election that night.*"

The outcome of this historical event clearly shows the importance of giving serious consideration to physical appearance and physical skills. As Webley points out, television changed the landscape on the importance of visible form (just as radio had done for audible form), which has been true of presidential debates since 1960. Every four years, reviews of these debates put a laser focus on the physical performance of the candidates. The take-away learning for those of us not running for president is to realize that even though our form may not be reviewed on national television, it doesn't mean we're not being "reviewed" by our own audiences. Bottom line: form matters, regardless of whether we think it's legitimate or fair.

Form depends most heavily on what people see and hear. As previously discussed, of the five physical senses (seeing, hearing, touching, smelling, and tasting), the behaviors people see and hear are the two senses people primarily use to achieve presence and convey their ideas, so they are the focus of the next two chapters. In the example of the Nixon-Kennedy debates, it was the visible skills that won the day for Kennedy, but audible skills are every bit as important, and get equal billing in this book.

The following chart provides a comprehensive list of the audible and visible behaviors people use to convey content.

ACTION REQUIRES BEHAVIOR

Auditory	Visual	Auditory and Visual
• Volume	• Facial Expressions	• Word choice
• Inflection	• Eye Contact	• Choice to write or speak
• Pronunciation	• Body Language	• Interruptions—physical and verbal
• Pace	• Physical Appearance	• Sentence Structure/Grammar
• Balance of Questions and Statements	• Physical Timing	
• Silence	• Setting	
• Auditory Timing	• Punctuation	
• Air TIme	• Length of a Written Message	

The "choices" above can be perceived as positive, neutral or negative...
choose thoughtfully.

Effective ways to capitalize on each behavior are described in the next two chapters—what to do, and what not to do. The chart shows the two broad communication categories: **audible behaviors** (what people hear), detailed in Chapter 14, and **visible behaviors** (what people see), detailed in Chapter 15.

The behaviors listed under each category identify the specific actions people use every day to communicate what's inside their heads. It's important to keep in mind that each behavior can be carried out in many, many ways. For example, "volume" includes every vocal nuance from a scream to a whisper. "Facial expressions" include an entire spectrum from smiles to frowns to scowls. The "length of a written message" could be a few words (perhaps a short e-mail or a note) or many pages of words (perhaps a long e-mail or a book). "Timing" can mean being early, on time, or late. These are just a few of the alternatives within each behavior choice that are covered. Knowing how to choose the best behaviors for your message is vital—they can be used to your advantage or abused at your peril.

The sense of touch is omitted from the chart because it has limited use in daily communication and isn't particularly skill-related. Inappropriate touching can indeed be a problem, but that concern isn't addressed here: for more information on this topic, please refer to the sexual harassment literature.

One behavior in the "touch" category worth mentioning, however, is the handshake. If your handshake needs improvement, you need to know. An overly aggressive grip can be physically painful for the receiver. Pumping away and not letting go is awkward. Forget fingertip shakes altogether. A limp, cold-fish contact is even worse. Get feedback from a trusted friend or colleague who can provide appropriate coaching to ensure your handshake is acceptable. Very few people are going to offer feedback if you don't ask. A properly executed handshake is an essential skill, because it's often one of the first impressions others have of us, and lots of people don't do it well. Be an exception.

It would be nice to think that people carefully choose the best behaviors to convey the content they want to share, but these "choices" are usually drawn from habits, occur spontaneously, and get executed without much conscious thought. If people knew the variety of behavioral alternatives available, and selected only the most suitable ones for a given situation, they would be more interesting and convincing.

Most of us don't have much awareness of the many ways our bodies and voices can either support communication or truly sabotage it—habits numb and desensitize us. People who haven't yet learned effective techniques, but think they have a good understanding of how to use their voices and bodies effectively, should probably think again. There is a big gap between a general understanding of the physical skills that enhance form, and the specific knowledge required to execute. Great communicators know this and use it to their full advantage. Because so few people have this awareness, they don't demonstrate good form. Their ineffective habits get in the way. It's almost certain you're unaware of any ineffective ones of your own, or you would have changed them by now. Right?

Habits, of course, are not bad in and of themselves. Some habits are good, like the times you automatically say "please" when asking for something. Habits are friends when they help us get through the day efficiently and quickly. Our brains are wired to favor efficiency over effort, so expect your brain to prefer habit-forming routines. Unfortunately, the brain doesn't easily differentiate between good and bad habits, so the ones that counteract our preferred outcomes become potent enemies. This is a perfect time to call on the brain function that fuels self-awareness (review Chapter 12) to purge bad habits and exchange them for new and improved versions.

Not surprisingly, most of us are often quite aware of other people's bad habits, while being blind to our own. This makes logical sense, because we can't see or accurately hear ourselves. It's important to realize that every sound or physical move we make has some kind of value—positive, neutral, or negative—to anyone who can see and hear us. Behavioral science literature says that many of our unconscious body movements provide information to others about what's going on inside our heads beyond what we verbalize. For example, looking down may imply we're lying, or crossing our arms may indicate discomfort. The book *What Every Body Is Saying* by Joe Navarro (HarperCollins Publishers, 2008) offers examples of many body movements, what they mean, and how to develop the skill to interpret those movements.

That said, some behavioral science literature suggests that deliberately managing our body movements indicates a lack of truthfulness. A simple example of this might be learning to develop a poker face to disguise a royal flush. I agree that many of our body movements, especially the automatic and subconscious ones, do potentially indicate some deeper meaning, but I don't agree that controlling them necessarily means we're not being truthful. Learning to control them can also mean we choose not to detract from our message. We understand that some body movements can be quite distracting, and choose instead to replace them with behaviors that support content. I want to emphasize that the advice in the next two chapters is given to enhance presence, not to learn how to outsmart people who read body language well.

Unfortunately, if you're doing something goofy with your voice or body, you'll probably be the last to know, unless you actively seek feedback. People don't commonly give feedback on the annoying mannerisms they observe in others—it's awkward and would feel impolite to say something, so people don't tell us. A few examples of visible bad habits include: fast-moving eyeballs, jiggling legs, drumming fingers, cracking knuckles, eating fast, slurping soup, walking like a duck, twirling or fussing with hair, making odd gestures, shifting weight from leg to leg, wearing out-of-place clothing, or sporting an odd hairstyle. A few audible bad habits include: speaking in a monotone, saying *ah* and *um* or *like* every other word, over-talking, under-talking, talking fast, using poor grammar, mispronouncing words, mumbling words, interrupting, laughing at the wrong time, snorting, or choosing inappropriate or offensive words. That paints a pretty picture, yes? And these bad habits are just the beginning of a very long list of distracting behavioral mannerisms or physical appearance gaffes committed around the globe each day. It doesn't take much people-watching time to build an interesting inventory.

Sadly, it's all too common for people to talk about our bad habits behind our backs. Consequently, we're seldom aware whether any odd mannerisms or appearance blunders are the star of our show, rather than content being the main event. On such occasions, our reputations are harmed—and we don't even know it.

To complicate matters, sometimes a specific behavior can be suitable in one circumstance but not in another, and it's useful to know when and where. For example, the slang that may be acceptable with close friends might be inappropriate if used in a work setting. People who bring their "hip talk" into the workplace often don't realize that it doesn't play well. Learning one set of habits that works everywhere would seem to be a more manageable choice, but anyone who can keep straight and pull off different ways of talking and behaving—based on the people they are with—should feel free to do so.

A word of caution: habits die hard. It can be painful to

break them. Substituting effective behaviors for the familiar, but ineffective, habits you've become accustomed to will take concentration and discipline. If you decide to make some behavior changes based on the advice presented here, be prepared to spend time practicing.

Reading about the skills is easy; executing new behaviors will be hard—so get ready. There will be moments when giving up and going back to the old ways will seem like a great idea. Some of your bad habits may take as long as a month to break, but stick with it. Persevere, and let that grit deep down inside you go to work. New behaviors will become habitual—sooner than you might imagine—and they will feel as comfortable as your current ineffective habits feel today. Remember, you're just replacing bad old habits with better new ones. You will comfortably return to autopilot again, but with physical habits that will support delivery of content rather than sabotage it. Each of us is unique, of course, so how long it takes for an individual to adapt new behaviors will depend on the level of dedication to the work. The ten case studies in Chapters 16 and 17 give ideas about how to integrate the skills into everyday life.

Increased awareness of oneself, others, and the environment simplifies choosing the best physical skills to get points across and, over time, develops the positive habits that contribute to good form. By doing so, the chances of being understood—just as we hope—significantly improves. Becoming more aware of others helps us notice the indirect feedback people are sending—facial expressions, tone of voice, and body language. It also provides information about our own content—is it getting through, or not? With immediate feedback, we can make immediate adjustments. Interactive communication like this is far more effective than operating in a vacuum.

A great way to increase awareness of others is when we're not part of the action. It's an opportunity to sit back and observe how people interact, allowing an evaluation of which behaviors work, and which ones don't. Take advantage of this stress-free way to pick up new skills. How easy or hard are these skills to learn? Here are my favorite definitions of *easy* and *hard*:

• It's easy when you know.
• It's hard when you don't.

A-a-a-ah, sounds simple, but oh so true. Don't feel discouraged if it's difficult to drop ineffective habits. That's to be expected. Any change is hard if we don't know what to do. And, of course, it's easy if we do. Just as some behaviors have enhanced your communication over the years, there are probably others that are not serving you very well. The information that follows provides precise and specific information to help you become more aware of behaviors that work, the ones that need fine-tuning, and what you need to abandon and rebuild from scratch. Enjoy *what's easy* for you and work on *what's hard*.

The skills discussed in the next two chapters are essential for overcoming Clueless Emperors, and they're also effective with Clued-In citizens. Learn these skills, and even if you miraculously never experience a shark on your tail for the rest of your life, you'll be a more effective communicator. Because of this, I'll reference Clueless Emperors only occasionally in the next two chapters. The skills described are life skills, and they work every day. Run, don't walk, to learn them, practice until they become habits, and use those new habits all the time. Don't save clear, effective, and even brilliant communication for Clueless Emperors alone. That would be a waste of talent.

Chapter 13 Main Points
The Behavioral Menu

- Our voices and bodies are the primary vehicles that convey content.
- Behavioral skills are crucial to overcoming Clueless Emperors.
- Behavioral skills work effectively in everyday communication.
- Showcase your content by avoiding odd mannerisms.
- People develop behavioral habits subconsciously.
- Behaviors can be consciously adjusted to enhance communication.

"The ability to persuade trumps the power to command."
—A Recovering Clueless Emperor

CHAPTER 14

Audible Behaviors of the Clued-In

"Words mean more than what is set down on paper. It takes the human voice to infuse them with deeper meaning."
—Maya Angelou

This chapter gives detailed descriptions of the audible behaviors that increase credibility, especially when you're in the thick of it with Clueless Emperors. Until now, you probably haven't thought much about how your voice can influence whether people find you interesting and believable—but at the end of this chapter, you will know what a great asset your voice can be in this regard. You'll boost awareness of current habits and learn how to improve the delivery of your message by optimizing how and when to use your vocal cords. The actual sounds of our voices—separate from content—carry not-so-subtle messages of their own, and it's what this section is all about.

Volume and Inflection. Although it's critical to understand volume and inflection as separate entities, they work in tandem. As audible skills go, achieving appropriate volume in everyday situations is usually pretty easy. Most of us have a good sense of how much volume to use in casual settings. Group settings are a different matter, but more about that in a moment. Regarding the use of your "everyday" voice, consistently speaking too softly (without realizing it, out of habit) or shouting (without realizing it, out of habit) are indicators that you have some work to do. Either way, it's likely that soft-spoken people have been asked to speak up (*"I can't hear you—what did you say?"*) or shouters have been asked to tone it down (*"No need to holler—I can hear you"*). If your volume is too low or too high, most people will let you know, at least indirectly. If no one has ever indicated these things to you, your everyday volume is probably appropriate. However, if you've received feedback along these lines and haven't acted on it, now would be a good time.

A particular circumstance where it's especially important to pay attention to volume is when you're irritated. The anger emotion gets the shark in your brain very excited, and finding the common sense to keep your volume in check can be challenging. If your common sense wins this battle, however, it's nothing short of amazing how effective low volume can be in such circumstances. Angry exchanges are often quickly brought under control when volume is controlled. This doesn't mean that low volume coupled with a sarcastic tone is excused. It's low volume with a neutral-to-considerate tone that works.

A common situation where people have trouble cali-brating appropriate volume is when they speak in front of a group. Not everyone has occasion to do this, but if you do, it's important to ensure volume is at the right level. Because many people feel uncomfortable in this setting, they mumble or speak too softly which conveys uncertainty. The appropriate volume in conversations is not enough for group presentations, because audience members won't be able to hear. Polls indicate that public speaking is people's number-one fear, even coming ahead of dying, and low volume is often the way this appre-hension manifests itself.

If you make presentations to groups, ask for feedback about volume. Never assume people who can't hear will let you know. Even as an audience member, when you have something to say—a town hall, PTA, or business meeting are examples—use appropriate volume. In these settings, how many times are questions asked that audience members can't hear? Getting a presenter's answer to a mystery question isn't useful.

A microphone adds volume, but it doesn't add inflection, and a booming monotone isn't compelling. If the room and group size are so large that vocal amplification is required and a microphone is available, be aware you'll need to increase inflection on your own. Along with increased volume, additional inflection is required for large group settings—and no one has invented an electronic device to do this for us. The inflection that's suitable for casual conversations isn't enough for large groups.

So what is inflection exactly? It involves simultaneous changes in volume and tone of voice that serve to emphasize words in order to convey specific meaning—examples of this are coming up. Inflection is highly nuanced and varies across languages and cultures, so keep in mind that the advice in this section is applicable to American English. If you're visiting a foreign country and using a translation guide, be aware that the inflection norms in your repertoire don't apply across languages.

In written form, we indicate word emphasis with punctuation or descriptive verbs or adverbs in dialogue tags. In audible form, inflection is achieved through our vocal cords and diaphragm. Changing tone of voice—from ironic, say, to sincere—also changes the meaning of content, just through a subtle tonal variation. As an example, experiment saying the word "please" using various volume levels and tones of voice to see how many different meanings you can generate.

Low-to-no inflection comes across as a monotone, which leaves it up to listeners to figure out the meaning of the message—there's no information beyond the words themselves for receivers to know specifically what the speaker has in mind. To complicate this, people on the other side of a boring monotone message are usually uncomfortable giving feedback—they don't want to be impolite—so speakers who don't capitalize on the gift of inflection usually don't know how they sound to others. Inflection can also go down the wrong emotional track and work against us—examples are angry or scolding tones—which is why inflection is important to manage. Its misuse, or lack of use, can interfere with intentions and content.

Let's look at an example of how changes in inflection can alter the meaning of a simple message. The following sentences have the identical words in identical order. The only difference among them is that different words are emphasized (through inflection) as they are spoken. The words in boldface indicate a slight increase in volume and a change in vocal tone. The questions in parentheses after each sentence indicate how most people would interpret each sentence if it was spoken with a vocal emphasis on the bolded word:

- **I** didn't say Mary brought the book. (Someone else said it?)
- I didn't say **Mary** brought the book. (Someone else brought it?)
- I didn't say Mary **brought** the book. (Did she send it?)
- I didn't say Mary brought the **book**. (She brought something else?)

These examples show that inflection alone can significantly alter meaning—no word changes required. How could these words be interpreted as the speaker intends if they were spoken without inflection? It's why low-to-no inflection is at the heart of so many misunderstandings.

A monotone is never effective unless the goal is to fade into a wall. When people speak in a monotone, they probably don't know, or they would certainly want to fix it. Listeners won't tell a speaker he or she is boring—it feels awkward or confrontational. Most listeners want to be "polite." They'll just tune out instead, or send text messages when they're not listening. Or sometimes they use the indirect feedback approach, close their eyes, and fall asleep.

How do we achieve inflection that captures attention? If this were an audio book, I could demonstrate, but I'll use descriptive words instead to show how meaning can be conveyed through tone of voice:

- "Mary brought the book," she *whimpered.*
- "It was Mary who brought the book!" he *shouted.*
- "Mary, please bring the book," her father *pleaded.*

The verbs "whimpered," "shouted," and "pleaded" indicate tone of voice and provide information about the speaker's emotional state. Experiment with your voice (in private) to get accustomed to the various tones that best support the meaning of what you want to say. Record your practice sessions and listen. It's essential to take full advantage of vocal cords and diaphragm—appropriate tone of voice supports content and adds interest. Of course, the specific words chosen are important too, but well-managed inflection can change an ordinary communication into an extraordinary one.

Inflection or emphasis used inappropriately can also damage a message. Sarcasm, for example, is rarely helpful unless it's done with obvious humor, at the right moment with the right audience. It's best to avoid inflection that communicates any form of anger (frustration, irritation, and exasperation are examples), unless that particular feeling is precisely what's intended. It's always beneficial to remember that most people don't respond well to shark bites. Also keep in mind that "sarcasm" and "anger" are perceptions, and speakers don't have the final say on how their tone is interpreted—their listeners do. Just because you didn't mean to sound sarcastic or angry doesn't mean you won't be heard that way. It's a good idea to steer clear of tones along these lines to avoid nasty repercussions. The 8-out-of-10 rule is useful to think about in this regard. Clueless Emperors don't like angry tones any more than anyone else does and will use their power to thrash anyone who uses it with them. They, of course, feel free to use it them-selves at their whim, because they can. It gives them a sense of control—their favorite state of being.

If you're wondering about the quality of your own inflec-tion, ask a few trusted friends for feedback. Five people or so should provide a large enough sample size for a balanced view. Some people you ask may not fully understand what inflection is (after all, we pay much more attention to content than form), so take the time to explain it—the feedback you get will be more helpful.

A good-quality audio recording will also help you learn more about your voice. How we sound through our own ears is usually quite different from how we sound to others. As an example, a common inflection error is using an uptick in pitch at the end of declarative sentences. This change in inflection is appropriate for questions, but using it with declarative sentences makes the speaker sound unsure, and comes across as sing-songy. Women seem to do this more often than men in my experience. Questions should be differentiated from declarative statements through the use of appropriate inflec-tion.

As you can see (or hear, in this case), inflection and volume are important elements in communication. They influence how a message is interpreted and contribute to whether the speaker is perceived to be interesting. People who use low volume or low-to-no-to-inappropriate inflection are inviting Clueless Emperors who don't like their ideas to take a bite out of them, so make sure yours are outstanding.

Main Points of Volume and Inflection:
- Get feedback to ensure volume is well-calibrated for any given situation.
- People commonly don't use enough volume or inflection when speaking to large groups.
- Be aware that a change in inflection alone can change the meaning of a message.
- A monotone voice is not only boring, but also makes it easy for listeners to misinterpret or ignore the speaker.

Pronunciation and Pace. Pronunciation has two components: enunciation and accent. Each one takes time and practice to change if a modification is desired. Of the two, enunciation usually carries more weight regarding how a person is perceived—this can be positive or negative depending on the quality of the enunciation. As an example, when syllables of words aren't fully articulated, people hear mumbling, making it difficult to understand the content of the message. Fair or not, a person who enunciates this way might be viewed as uneducated. "*Ya hafta wanna*" might be acceptable in the mall chatting with friends or solving world problems over coffee, but in order to be clearly understood, say it this way: "*You have to want to.*" Articulating each syllable of every word too precisely might make a person sound like a stuffed shirt. The ideal is finding the proper middle ground between sloppy enunciation and overly precise enunciation. The primary goal is to have people understand what was said the first time without needing to ask the speaker to repeat. Audio recordings and feedback provide clues if you want to know how people hear you.

The second component of pronunciation has to do with regional accents. Everyone has a regional accent, and some of them are more colorful than others. People who have strong regional accents and speech patterns that draw attention need to decide whether they're making negative, neutral, or positive impressions. Some people have prejudices against strong accents: "redneck" or "surfer dude" talk are examples. These prejudices aren't right or fair, but they are a reality. Accents vary widely, and people who have them sometimes get labeled—from dull or dimwitted to arrogant or snobbish. If the way you talk detracts from what you want to communicate—in other words, an accent becomes the main event in place of content—a change might be in order. Dialect coaches can help if this is a concern for you.

The pace at which we speak also plays an important role in effective communication. If pace falls outside the normal curve and is on the "too fast" side, listeners may not be able to keep track of what's being said. They will likely have to ask the speaker to slow down so they can understand. But "too slow" is less likely to elicit feedback—most listeners would feel uncomfortable acknowledging their boredom, though they may nod off while the speaker talks.

It's difficult to be objective and accurately evaluate our own speech patterns, so if you even slightly suspect that your pace is too fast or too slow, get direction from a professional coach. In lieu of a coach, feedback from competent friends and colleagues is also helpful, or make an audio recording and dispassionately evaluate what you hear. Pronunciation and pace are deeply habitual and difficult to change. For example,

actors who play roles requiring a dialect or foreign accent sometimes require months of professional coaching before filming
or going on stage. The average individual rarely needs a
complete overhaul, but even slight adjustments can be challenging. If you have problems with pronunciation or pace and
also speak too softly, no one is likely to understand anything
you say. If a Clueless Emperor comes along while you're
mumbling or murdering the language, you will be ignored.

Main Points of Pronunciation and Pace:
- Pronunciation includes regional accents and
  enunciation.
- Pronunciation is deeply habitual and difficult to
  change.
- Sometimes even slight adjustments in pronunciation
  can make a big difference.
- Pace that is too fast or too slow needs to be
  adjusted.

Word Choice When Speaking. Most of us speak more
often than we write. When there is a choice, people usually
verbalize what they want to communicate because it's fast and
efficient. Unless we're being recorded or someone is taking
verbatim notes, what we say is usually short-lived. This means
spoken words, by and large, have comparatively less influence
than written words—people will more quickly forget what they
hear than what they read. There are exceptions, of course:
speeches made in formal settings, or when the speaker is
famous, or when someone has a cell phone and our words turn
up on public sites like YouTube. Then everybody pays attention.
As an example, words can turn negative when they pass through
the local gossip grapevine or get memorialized on the internet.
It's why choosing appropriate words when we speak is a crucial

skill. A lot of the advice in this section also applies to written words, and you'll read even more about how to be an influential writer in the next chapter.

Clued-In citizens are aware that words have two components: a denotation (the dictionary definition), and a connotation (an implied inference related to the context in which the word is used). This means that in addition to the dictionary definition, words also carry emotional subtexts that have positive, negative, or neutral implications. It's best to consider both denotation and connotation when deciding how you want to say what's on your mind. Words with similar meanings can communicate very different things, depending on the setting and situation. As an example, the type of language we use chatting with a friend may not work with the boss. Words that work with the boss may not necessarily be successful with children.

The English language, with its extensive and complex vocabulary, has many words with similar meanings which makes it challenging to make good choices for any given circumstance. Even words that are synonymous aren't identical in meaning. There are differences (connotations) among them—they aren't freely interchangeable because shades of meaning separate them. To complicate this, the same word that's said using different inflections can also convey different meanings (see examples in the "Volume and Inflection" section in this chapter).

Let's consider an example of some synonymous words, all having a negative connotation: *foolish, silly, asinine, witless, insane,* and *preposterous.* Even though these words have similar meanings, can they be used interchangeably? Of course they cannot—there are shades of differences among them. This is why we have to consider and evaluate how most people (apply the 8-out-of-10 rule here) will interpret the words we choose.

If you've ever said something and immediately wanted to take it back, it's a sign you chose the wrong words.

Always pay attention to the environment, and anyone nearby who may be able to hear you. Use straightforward and appropriate words, not ambiguous or unsuitable words, for your message. If you want to change something you've said (Clueless Emperors are immune from this feeling), it's generally acceptable in the moment. Exceptions are sound bites that go viral—people don't easily forget or forgive explosive or loaded words said in anger. Words carry an emotional element that can't be separated from content, which is why it's so important to choose words that clearly express what is intended.

Spoken words are usually not consciously selected, but more often chosen in a split second instead. Spontaneously blurting whatever comes to mind in the moment sometimes gets people into trouble. When the words you're getting ready to say are especially important to "get right" the first time, take care with your choices. Pause briefly and think carefully before you speak in these circumstances. A message that comes across as antagonistic or disrespectful won't be excused by 8-out-of-10 people. If you're known to have a quick temper, or commonly shoot off your mouth, and haven't done anything to fix it, *now* would be a great time. Get help if necessary. There are many resources available, and no excuses for doing nothing about it.

Words that convey anger carry a price tag. Let's say a teenage boy bullies one of his friends, which shocks and appalls his parents. Some strong words probably flash through the parents' minds as they confront their son, but once angry words are spoken, they're not easily taken back. Helping the boy understand that bullying is not acceptable requires effective instruction; the words for any kind of coaching have to be chosen carefully. Calling their son a bully, even if it's true, will probably not help him learn appropriate behavior—in such a case, the parents are behaving like Clueless Emperors, using their position power foolishly. Asking questions about the incident and providing alternate approaches to controlling anger will yield better results than a lecture. This kind of teaching is an effective way to role model interpersonal skills. Preaching, nagging, lecturing, and yelling do not work—they never have, and they never will. Good coaching is built on a foundation of awareness, so it's important to become skilled in this area. Chapter 12 provides a good refresher.

Notice how words affect listeners. For example, what does a hurt expression on someone's face imply? Or someone's backside as he does an about-face and walks away? Or a big smile? These are example of nonverbal feedback that require thoughtful consideration. Pay attention to how people respond to your words by observing their behavior. And then make deliberate decisions about what to do with that information.

On a much lighter note, the "last word" on word choice is about non-words. These are the filler sounds or repeated words such as *ah, um, like, I mean, y'know*, and other variations on that theme. I have to say, it drives me crazy when I hear them. People who use these annoying and unnecessary fillers must not realize they're doing it—who would do this intentionally? Some completely clueless people use them multiple times in every sentence they speak. Even though these non-word verbal tics are often heard subconsciously, it doesn't mean they don't register with receivers: listeners aren't persuaded by what they hear—they just can't say specifically why not.

Useless sounds or unnecessary words are distracting, will never help communication, and will likely hurt it. They come in various and unusual forms, so there isn't a rule book that specifically spells out everything to avoid. A past client had an especially unusual filler—she made a slight laughing sound at the end of most of her sentences—which came across as though she didn't expect to be taken seriously, or perhaps that she didn't take herself seriously. She wasn't conscious of doing this until she signed up for an evaluation of her communication behaviors. When I called the habit to her attention, she was instantly conscious, and in very little time put a stop to it. Awareness is a wonderful thing.

An audio recording may help you become aware of any fillers or non-words in your speech pattern, but enlist an objective person who will listen to the playback with you—it's sometimes difficult to pick up on our own mistakes.

Main Points of Word Choice When Speaking:
- Synonyms have similar meanings that aren't precisely the same, so they aren't freely interchangeable.
- Words have emotional components that should be considered when deciding what to say.
- Non-words are annoying sounds and unnecessary fillers (such as *ah, um, like, y'know*) that reduce a speaker's influence.
- Clueless Emperors have an advantage when their challengers don't choose words carefully.

Balance of Questions and Declarative Statements. Have you ever wondered whether you ask enough questions? It's normal to use more declarative statements than questions in everyday speech, but most people overdo it on the declarative side. By doing so, they subtly but clearly imply their interest in wanting *you* to know what *they* think, even if their silence would have been a better choice. Asking questions presumes an interest in knowing what others have to say. It's that simple.

Asking questions fosters collaboration, indicates curiosity, and builds trust. In addition, asking questions is connected to the dynamic of people *liking to be right,* which was covered in Chapter 9. People enjoy giving answers, because it provides the dopamine rush of being right … at least for a minute or two. We can use this information to our advantage. *Asking questions can build and strengthen relationships. Who knew?* Asking questions and listening to responses are key factors in any collaboration or problem-solving mission. Most people love to be asked questions, especially Clueless Emperors, because "having the answer" is their reason for living. It's a great tactic to use when you want to overcome them. They talk on and on, usually repeating themselves, giving *you* time to think. An added benefit: this skill is in short supply, and a relatively easy habit to develop.

In the past few years, collaboration (which is a perception, not a behavior) has been touted as a business imperative in several corporate and government organizations. It's become a popular buzz word commonly listed as a goal or objective in the mission statements and values declarations in many of these organizations. I'm all for collaboration, but merely recording it in an organizational document doesn't mean it's going on. People who truly want collaboration need to ensure collaborative behaviors are defined, taught, and rewarded. Reinforcing the use of questions is a good place to start.

For example, most of us experienced the consequences of the global economic devastation that began in 2008. Collaboration was certainly in short supply leading up to the downfall, even though people who could have prevented the catastrophe would probably have been the first to *say* they believed in collaborative methods. In perhaps oversimplified terms, a critical mass of selfish people used their intellects to invent creative economic formulas to serve themselves. They weren't collaborating with anyone. Why would these same people have advocated for collaboration? Because it's politically correct to say so, and therefore has sound-bite appeal. Would-be advocates of "collaboration" throw this word around without *behaviorally demonstrating* they themselves are willing to try it, let alone have the ability to do it. This causes the people who depend on them, their potential collaborators, to become skeptical at best, and victims of excessive ambition at worst.

Advocating the benefits of collaboration and not following through with corresponding actions doesn't fool anyone. When words and actions don't match, people notice the lack of integrity and stop trusting. The self-focus that characterizes Clueless Emperors causes them to do a lot of telling and not much asking. Any chance they may have had to gain respect begins to erode with this behavior. They don't notice that people are placating or perhaps even avoiding them. It's common to be cautious around Clueless Emperors, so people may give lip service ... but then shy away from any opportunities to speak up. It's just too risky.

Skillful collaboration, on the other hand, encourages openness. One of the best ways to collaborate, of course, is to *ask questions*, and not the rhetorical kind. Ask questions that demand real answers and listen to how people respond. Then ask more questions and listen to those answers, too. Rhetorical questions are useful in some situations, but not when collaboration is the goal. With collaboration, questions need to be rooted in curiosity. Asking questions for the purpose of getting information promotes authentic discussion.

We've all been asked to participate in conversations or meetings with the stated purpose of generating ideas or openly discussing an issue. If the initiators of these conversations are Clueless Emperors who do all the talking, we wonder why they bothered to ask for input. If collaboration is desired, the initiators have to ask questions, and the participants have to be given time to respond. If the initiators want to build trust, they have to listen to the information they receive and consider the merits of the ideas being offered.

There isn't a magic formula for the right number of questions to ask (in a ratio to the number of declarative statements) in any given conversation or discussion. Each situation calls for a different balance. As an example, it's more appropriate for subject-matter experts giving presentations to do most of the talking, using declarative sentences. On the other hand, when someone conducts a meeting where the purpose is gathering ideas from participants, it's important for the leader to take a low-key role and facilitate the discussion. Here the initiator does more asking and listening instead of declaring and talking.

Do you need to ask more questions? Start counting the number of questions you ask in your everyday conversations. A bit of multi-tasking is required for this exercise: you need to silently keep track of questions while maintaining a focus on content. If you're currently not asking many questions, it may be difficult to think of any to ask—take this take as an indication of a bad habit that needs to be reformed: too much telling has been going on. Another common bad habit you may self-discover from this exercise—focusing on what to say next, rather than actively listening to what is being said.

Main Points of Balance of Questions and Declarative Statements:
- Most people don't ask enough questions. Be an exception.
- Asking questions fosters collaboration.
- After posing questions, give thoughtful consideration to answers.

Silence. Yes, remaining silent is a behavior. You can choose not to speak. And sometimes silence really is golden. Not speaking isn't the same as listening, however, and it's important to know the difference. When two people are in conversation, one can be silent, look at the person speaking, nod, and give all appearances of listening—and still not hear a word. Conversely, while someone is talking, the receiver can be multi-tasking (texting, e-mailing, staring off into space and seeming not to listen) and still take in everything that's being said. It's not possible to know whether people are listening from their behavior alone, although silence is often interpreted as a positive sign of listening. If you want to be thought of as a good listener, being silent is a good place to start. But more than silence is required.

How can we assess whether someone is listening? Use this technique: *ask a question related to the subject matter of what you've said.* Let's say you're speaking on a topic and want to ensure that receivers understand. Ask something like, "What do you think about this issue?" The reply will verify whether listeners were paying attention. Even the best of us tune out occasionally, so when it's important to know if listeners are taking in what has been said, use this technique to verify you're communicating clearly. Of course, you'll want to use a tone of voice that indicates curiosity, not a tone that embarrasses or challenges—that's what Clueless Emperors do.

Remember the story about Over-Talker-Gary in Chapter 12? I chose complete silence to help him become aware of dominating the conversation. This tactic seemed not to have had any effect during his actual monologue, but he *did* ask on our way out the door whether he had talked too much. I suspect my silence may have raised his consciousness enough to at least ask that question.

Silence is also a wonderful way to get input from people who aren't forthcoming with information. Most people don't tolerate silence very well, even when it lasts only a few seconds or so. They want to fill in any quiet spaces with noise, so they keep talking. We see the police and lawyers on TV using prolonged silence during interrogations to encourage people to open up. This approach often gets them the information they want.

Assume for a moment that you're in conversation with someone who is withholding information or otherwise not being responsive. Try remaining silent while keeping a pleasant facial expression, perhaps raising your eyebrows to indicate interest. This technique works especially well with children. People sometimes appreciate getting a bit of silent space in which to think. But more commonly, people start talking to fill the quiet void, revealing details you might not otherwise have been given. Silence is also quite effective when Clueless Emperors are on the attack. They tend to run off at the mouth, which allows time to assess their intentions and collect thoughts for a return volley. Don't try to get a word in while they're ranting—it doesn't help, and they won't hear you anyway.

Although not impossible, it's difficult to listen and talk at the same time—another reason silence is advantageous. People who talk over each other aren't communicating, they're venting. Don't ever waste time doing this.

When you yourself are doing the talking, capitalize on the benefits of silence by pausing. The pauses can be quite brief, say, as short as a couple of seconds. It provides thinking time for the speaker and gives listeners time to digest what's been said.

Main Points of Silence:
- Silence and listening are not the same thing.
- Most people would rather talk than listen, so avoid falling into this trap. Use silence deliberately.

• Staying silent while collecting thoughts increases credibility.
• Talking over people is a waste of time.

Auditory Timing. The moment we decide to speak or make any kind of sound, such as laughing or sighing, we're demonstrating a behavior known as timing. Speaking or making a sound can be viewed positively, neutrally, or negatively depending on the situation. Here are some examples:

• Laughter is positive when someone says something funny at no one's expense. It's negative when the laughter comes at an inappropriate moment, or comes across as sarcastic or demeaning.
• Talking over someone is usually viewed as aggressive and is perceived negatively.
• Answering a question promptly when asked is usually perceived positively.
• Snorting or making other rude noises after someone has made a comment is perceived negatively.
• Clapping is judged positively when it occurs at the end of a performance or speech. It's perceived negatively when it occurs after someone has done something inappropriate.
• Crying or sighing can be perceived negatively or positively, depending on circumstances.

It's important to be aware that whatever sounds we make, the timing of those sounds communicates a message of its own. Even breathing can be noticeable and carry meaning, especially if it's labored. Almost any "noise" will draw people's attention, so make sure any sound you make draws the desired attention. As an example, blurting out thoughts the moment they hit us might imply we're anxious or nervous, even though that may not be true.

Interrupting is a common form of auditory timing. It's generally acceptable to interrupt occasionally with a tone of voice that isn't hostile or demeaning, but is pleasant or enthusiastic instead. Done infrequently and with a warm tone of voice, the interrupter may well be viewed as engaged, in a positive way. A demeaning tone of voice or frequent interruptions are not acceptable. Occasionally it becomes important to interrupt, especially with people who dominate conversations, but use this tactic judiciously. Interrupting Clueless Emperors sometimes causes shark bites, so exercise sound judgment while they are blathering.

Main Points of Auditory Timing:
- Making any kind of sound is an example of timing.
- Any sound you make will usually draw people's attention.
- Sounds and spoken words should be chosen consciously, not used accidentally.
- Interrupt judiciously and use a pleasant tone of voice.

The Choice to Write or Speak. Deciding whether to write or speak a message is a behavioral option. Most of the time it's an obvious choice. Here are three oversimplified examples to make the point:

- People are gathered in one place at the same time, so communication is most easily achieved through talking rather than passing notes.
- A sign is posted to advertise a garage sale because it's more efficient than communicating the message by going door to door in person.

• A question received by e-mail is usually most easily answered with e-mail.

The decision whether to write or speak a message usually isn't a difficult one. We don't have to ponder what the best choice would be very often. There are occasions, however, when a decision could legitimately go either way. For example, let's say a guideline about a new procedure needs to be given to a group of people. If the guideline is simple, and all who need to know are together in the same vicinity, verbalizing it may be the most appropriate choice. This option also allows time for questions on the spot. If the guideline is technical, it might be more practical to put it in writing so receivers have a chance to carefully review and digest the information. With technical data, sending a written document that can be used for reference is often preferred.

Any situation requires a thoughtful decision about how the message will be best understood. Both content and emotion should be considered. Sometimes written messages such as corporate memos or printed e-mails serve as necessary documentation, but other times such notes are seen as CYA (Cover Your Ass) missiles. Never write messages that serve the purpose of blaming—and even worse, copy lots of people to make a point.

The choice to verbalize a message is efficient and may feel warmer to the receiver, or it may come across that the speaker was too lazy to put the information into written form if the content is technical in nature. Carefully choose the right vehicle for every communication by assessing how it will be received.

Main Points of the Choice to Write or Speak:
• Make a deliberate decision about whether to write or speak when you have something to communicate.

- Complicated technical messages are best delivered in writing.

Air Time. Most of us spend more time talking than writing, so the air time any single person consumes is an important choice. What does air time mean in this context? Air time is the specific length of time a person talks during a conversation or discussion. Air time is "computed" by listeners in two ways: 1) how long is any one "speech," and 2) what is the overall compiled talk time each individual consumes. Unless there is a good reason for doing so, when someone uses up the majority of available air time, those who don't get an opportunity to participate will likely be annoyed. Useful information exchange usually fails in these situations. We've all been in conversations or meetings where an air-time hog has done most of the talking, and everyone *except* that person seemed aware of it. This insufferable nattering happens often, and the over-talker committing the air-time infraction is usually oblivious of the violation.

Try to be innocent of this breach in etiquette by using a default formula to determine a fair share of air time. Count the people involved in any conversation, discussion, or meeting and divide one hundred by that number. The answer is the percentage of available air time each participant can legitimately claim as his or her fair share. For example, if there are five people in a conversation, each participant gets twenty percent. If there are twenty people, each participant gets five percent, and so on. Enforcing a specific percentage of air time per person is not the point of this formula, however. It's a guideline. The goal is for each person to get his or her fair share roughly right in order to behave in Clued-In style.

Using one's entire fair share of air time all at once poses a problem, unless the interaction itself is of short duration. For example, imagine four friends enjoying a one-hour lunch together. The fair share of air time per person would be fifteen minutes. It's easy to imagine, however, if one of the participants talked non-stop for fifteen minutes, he or she would probably not be invited to lunch again. Each participant's air time portion needs to be broken up. An exception would be a short, let's say two-minute, conversation among four people. If any one individual took his thirty-second allowance all at once, that would be appropriate.

There may be unique circumstances that dictate a different approach. As an example, when formally presenting to a group, the speaker at the front of the room justifiably gets most of the allotted air time because of her role as the subject-matter expert and presenter in that interaction. Another example might be an attempt to overcome a Clueless Emperor who doesn't stop talking. In such a situation, let the Emperor ramble on for a bit and think you're a genius for being an "appreciative" listener. Without such special circumstances such as these, however, it's best to focus on making the best use of your fair share of air time.

In a presentation with an established time limit, say fifteen minutes, to be followed by discussion, say thirty minutes, be aware that sticking to the schedule is important. A common violation of this guideline occurs when the presenter runs over the designated time, limiting the opportunity for discussion afterward and frustrating the attendees. Even though the presenter may be "sorry" after the fact, it doesn't mollify anyone. It's usually perfectly fine for an attendee to skillfully remind the speaker of the agenda's time limits. Just don't do this with an especially powerful Clueless Emperor—a public confrontation of that sort may end with a shark attack.

When you have a question, ask it crisply—no rambling without end. Call-in talk shows supply good examples of how annoying air-time hogs can be. The skills in this book provide tactics to gracefully enter and exit a discussion or conversation, so no need to monopolize the air time for fear of not fully expressing yourself.

If you're an air-time hog, I hope that's not happening intentionally. If so, work on adjusting to a fair share immediately. If not, you might as well wear a T-shirt advertising your Clueless Emperor status. Whether you're taking too much air time knowingly or not, pay close attention to how much talking you usually do, and determine whether it's within the guidelines of acceptability. Most people develop air-time habits, so be conscious of what yours are.

If an air-time hog can't be avoided, skillfully delivered developmental feedback is in order. Those who don't feel up to this task—because developmental feedback ability is not yet a strength—may want to find a skilled helper to deliver that message to avoid getting a shark bite.

Being noticeably quiet can also be a problem. If you have something to say, be assertive and say it. If anyone in a discussion takes less than his or her fair share of talk time in a given interaction, someone else is liable to pick up the slack. It's not fair, but people who routinely choose to take less than their fair share of air time may be viewed as unassertive, or even submissive. If that is your choice, understand that some people may question your ability. Under-talkers experience negative labels just like over-talkers do. That's why getting the air-time share just right is a benefit.

Main Points of Air Time:
- Calculate your fair share of air time and stay within that parameter unless circumstances dictate otherwise.
- The amount of air time taken by individuals sends a not-so-subtle message to others in the conversation—it shows a preference for control, retreat, or equality.

The Audible Bottom Line

This completes the detailed descriptions of the audible behaviors required for successful communication, especially when you need to overcome Clueless Emperors, or want to avoid being one yourself. There are many behaviors to keep in mind, and they're all important. Assess where you need a skill upgrade and work on desired improvements one at a time, so you won't feel overwhelmed.

Let's say you've selected three areas needing attention: increasing air time (because you have valuable ideas you sometimes keep to yourself), inflection (because you speak in a monotone), and pronunciation (because people consistently ask you to repeat what you've said). Working on all three of these skill areas at the same time may not be practical. Concentration is required to change behaviors, and it's not easy, or realistic, to focus on several skills simultaneously and be successful. Work on one goal at a time, achieve your objective, and move on to the next skill.

It may be useful to think about the combination of auditory skills and how they work together by imagining a concert. If we heard a solo performance with only one instrument or one voice in a musical composition written for a chorus or orchestra, it wouldn't sound complete. The intended effect of the musical piece would be noticeably lacking. When all the instruments or voices are combined, the music becomes fuller, more satisfying, and compelling. So it is with the total package of audible communication skills: our communication becomes fuller, more satisfying, and compelling.

A person skilled at word choice, but ineffective at asking enough questions, has work to do. Someone else might be great with enunciation but talks too fast, so there is work to do. Whatever "instruments" are missing from your skill orchestra, the deficiency will detract from the potential enjoyment of the symphony performance. Make a plan based on improving areas where you need development. Get to work, and you will soon feel the thrill of being a more effective communicator.

> *"Did I really say it that way? With those words?*
> *What was I thinking?"*
> —A Recovering Clueless Emperor

CHAPTER 15

Visible Behaviors of the Clued-In

"When people show you who they are, believe them."
—Maya Angelou

Now that you're clued-in to the skills that optimize your voice, it's time to learn about the behaviors people see—and how to capitalize on appearance and physical skills in the best possible way. The behaviors people exhibit influence how credible they seem, and whether their messages are received as intended. Of course, it's essential to have an impressive presence when interacting with Clueless Emperors—they chew up and spit out content if it's not delivered with good form. What follows is a comprehensive inventory of visible behavior and appearance options and how to use them to your advantage. Follow the recommendations, and physical presence will be enhanced allowing content to shine.

Facial Expressions. Does everyone interpret facial expressions in the same way? How are facial expressions and emotion connected? Do facial expressions add or detract from a message? These are commonly asked questions about the ways our faces wordlessly communicate. Research tells us that facial expressions subtly transmit information well beyond the words we speak. Hard and fast rules that guarantee how a particular arrangement of facial muscles will be interpreted don't exist, but there are behaviors that will improve the odds of being understood as intended.

Our faces are always communicating *something*. We involuntarily arrange our facial muscles constantly, and their various compositions can reveal a countless number of emotions. If we want to know whether facial expressions accurately reflect our intent, getting feedback from the people who see us provides clues. If we want to know whether we're interpreting other people's expressions in the way they intend, we need to discover a graceful way to find out. This issue was partially addressed in Chapter 11, "Using Emotion Effectively." I'll expand on it here and explain how facial expressions and emotions are connected, and what can be done to ensure they are compatible.

Let's imagine a meeting with several people, including Tom and Joan. At a point in the discussion when Joan is speaking, she sees an expression on Tom's face that she interprets to mean he has a question. If she's right, she might think Tom doesn't understand something she has said. Because she is a Clued-In citizen and doesn't want to make this assumption without asking, she can say something like, "Tom, it looks like you might have a question on this topic?" She knows that pleasantly checking out her assumption will encourage his participation and increase the likelihood that Tom will feel positively toward her. Conversely, if Joan were to state her interpretation as a fact using a clipped tone of voice—as in, "Tom, what is it you don't understand?"—he may feel put on the spot. Same interpretation of Tom's facial expression, two very different ways of asking him about it. A respectful approach works best, assuming there isn't a desire to intimidate, which is what Clueless Emperors do. Clued-In citizens know better than to behave selfishly or foolishly.

As noted in the previous chapter, tone of voice is also

important. If Joan's tone and facial expression were to indicate frustration that Tom wasn't keeping up—what if she asked with low volume, a sigh, and an eye roll thrown in?—Tom would probably be embarrassed, or perhaps even offended. On the other hand, if she uses a warm tone, looks directly at Tom, and adds a smile, he will likely be grateful she respectfully noticed his confusion.

Along with the words we use, facial expressions can increase a receiver's comfort level and participation. Conversely, a condescending facial expression (as perceived by 8-out-of-10 people) can shut down communication, even when the actual spoken words are the same in both scenarios. The challenge is that the behaviors we display are more often a result of reflex—out of habit—than by choice, which is why self-awareness provides advantages. Most people don't consciously distinguish between form and content—they've never been taught the difference—and anyone without this knowledge suffers the consequences. Like it or not, *how* people communicate through their facial expressions carries weight.

Here's an example of making that distinction, and what can be done to improve communication: Mom asks her son to come home right after school because he has a dentist appointment. She sees a look on his face that she interprets to mean he wants to go anywhere *except* to the dentist. The way she confirms her son's cooperation has the potential to be persuasive, or not. Asking him to verbalize that he'll be home on time is a better strategy than Mom herself reminding him a dozen times. Using the first approach verifies he understands and better enlists his commitment to follow through. It also prevents him from later saying he misunderstood. This way, Mom's "content" (getting her son to the dentist) has a better chance of getting through.

Another way to check the interpretation of a facial expression is to say something like, "By the look on your face, it seems you're (*fill in the blank*). Am I reading you correctly?" The answer helps confirm or deny the guess and encourages an emotional connection. This technique of asking for clarification is usually productive because people send indirect feedback all the time, sometimes unknowingly, so it's good to confirm what's going on. It gives receivers the opportunity to either verify they understand the emotional part of the message, or makes it clear they did not. Most people appreciate when we notice and inquire how they're doing.

Ask trusted colleagues and friends for feedback on your facial expressions. Are the words you say and the expressions on your face in or out of sync? As an example, have you ever been in a great mood when someone asks if you're having a bad day? We don't always know what our facial expressions communicate. To ensure our emotions are correctly inter-preted, verbalizing a felt emotion can help. Let's say, for example, that someone is talking on a topic he's passionate about. Saying something like, "I hope you can see how *excited* I am about this idea!" adds meaning to clarify content. If he happens not to *look* excited, his audience is at least getting a clue about how he feels through his words. Here are more examples with the felt emotion in bold:

> "I'm **worried** whether we're making the right decision."
> "I'm **sad** to see you go."
> "I'm **glad** you passed the test."
> "I'm **frantic** that we'll miss the flight."
> "I'm **disappointed** you didn't come to the meeting."
> "I'm **thrilled** you will be joining us on the trip."

It's best when words and facial expressions complement each other. If they don't correlate, we're sending mixed messages. Some skilled listeners may point this out, but we can't count on it. If they don't, it's easy to imagine they're privately questioning our integrity instead. Here's an example: let's say you invite a friend to a party, and you *privately* really want her to come, but she *privately* misreads your facial expression to mean you hope she declines. Knowing the liking-to-be-right tendency we all enjoy, your friend may turn her interpretation into a fact, and not feel very good about your invitation. If she doesn't give any outward indication she feels that way, you're left in the dark. As an alternative, if you add something like, "I would be so happy if you were free that evening, because there are people coming I want you to meet," there would be more clarity. These words help ensure you won't be misinterpreted. That's why it's helpful to verbalize felt emotions. By doing so, people have more than facial expressions to go by.

The various ways words are interpreted can't be guaranteed—after all, people make interpretations based on their own set of filters and biases—so it's important to think of this technique as an insurance policy that improves understanding. Even though the 8-out-of-10 rule is dependable, we should remember it's not called the 10-out-of-10 rule.

When Clueless Emperors are in an intimidating mood, outwardly acknowledging their behavior and linking it to emotion can disarm them—it spoils their bullying fun. Watch how they retreat if a Clued-In citizen can skillfully address their misconduct. A simple and neutrally stated comment (paying attention to tone of voice) like, "It seems you're angry about this," may be all it takes. The Emperor will probably deny it, but it will likely calm him down. Bad behavior often escalates unless someone calls attention to it.

When people focus solely on content, they lose sight of the powerful emotional influence their behaviors have on a message. If emotions are ignored, it's likely the chances of a winning result will decrease. Let's imagine you and I are discussing a relatively non-emotional topic, but my facial expression is conveying that I'm upset. You may be distracted to the point of not paying attention to the literal content and wonder what's going on with me instead. Or questioning why we're even having this conversation when something is emotionally affecting me. As discussed in Chapter 11, we know that many people often, and incorrectly, advise that content and emotion should be separated. This counsel is not only impractical, it's also not strategic. Acknowledging emotions creates opportunities for breakthrough communication. Emotions show themselves through our behavior in many ways—not the least of which is through facial expressions—and have an effect on our listeners, whether consciously or subconsciously.

Although facial expressions are interpreted similarly across different cultures around the world, there are exceptions, so don't assume. The acceptability of *showing* emotion definitely varies across cultures. Because norms differ, if you have questions about a particular region you're traveling to, do some homework before you depart on your journey.

Eye Contact. Eye contact and eye movement are elements of facial expressions, but they're worth special mention because of the significant role they play. All by themselves, they communicate unique messages of their own. In some cultures, looking directly at a person's face is considered overly bold and inappropriate. In Western culture, however, direct eye contact is considered a strength, so *good eye contact* in this section refers to Western cultural norms.

People who maintain good eye contact are usually viewed as interesting, confident, and attentive when such an interpretation may be far from the truth. Good eye contact can disguise nervousness and boredom; and poor eye contact can signal someone is shy, tense, or distracted, though the opposite may be true. Eye movements are deeply habitual, so whatever habits you've developed are probably unknown to you. It's crucial to have good eye contact, especially with Clueless Emperors when you're attempting to communicate with them. They're more likely to threaten people who look vulnerable—and you don't want to be one of those people. Give yourself a gift right now and assume your eye contact skills need help, but you don't know what the specific problems are—continue reading to get clues for improvement.

We often can't specify why a person doesn't seem credible or trustworthy, but the underlying cause is often related to bad eye contact. Eye movement usually registers only subconsciously with receivers: they quickly translate any bad-eye-contact behavior, and equate it with bad content (as discussed in Chapter 7). In these cases, even though content may be brilliant, the overall impression of the speaker is negative. It's the inability to differentiate between form and content that drives this miscalculation, and our strong cultural focus on content doesn't help.

Because a confident-looking presence is so important, and good eye contact is a big contributor to that appearance, I'll provide an eye movement formula that leaves a positive impression. If the eye movement pattern suggested here isn't what you already do, getting the formula integrated with your everyday behavior will feel quite awkward at first (*OK, very awkward*), so be prepared for some dedicated practice. The question to ask: is it better to keep a current bad habit and look awkward forever, or feel awkward for a while, using the suggested pattern, and look great forever?

Here's the formula: establish eye contact with each person you're talking to long enough to complete one thought (about five seconds), pause silently, turn to another person, establish eye contact again, and complete another thought. In highly interactive conversations, this might mean one thought to one person is all you get before someone else jumps into the conversation, and that's fine. Just be sure to pick a new person when your next turn to talk comes around. In other words, don't try to make eye contact with several people in one sentence with an eye sweep.

If there are three or more people in the group, be sure to include each of them in random order when you're doing the talking in order to avoid predictable eye movement. A common pitfall in these situations is to establish eye contact with only one person (as an example, imagine the boss is in the conversation) and ignore everyone else who is present. All listeners appreciate being included through eye contact, so the speaker should talk to each individual, one at a time, delivering one thought at a time. As a side benefit, this behavior also helps the speaker maintain focus. When eyes bounce around, so does thinking—the brain is flooded with visual data to process, and keeping thoughts on track becomes difficult. When people lose their train of thought, it's a good bet their eyes are not focused on talking to one person at a time.

All it takes is a few seconds to express a thought. It's the ideal amount of time to have eye contact and connect with a listener—long enough for each participant to feel included, and short enough to avoid a "stared at" feeling. With this technique, you'll come across as calm, knowledgeable, and thoughtful. Most people, however, move their eyes too quickly from person to person, making it hard for them to concentrate. Fast eye movements give a harried and flighty appearance. It's impossible to look at everyone at once, so don't try.

The same basic rule applies on a broader scale when speaking to a larger group. In this situation, it's especially important to look at people in random order, not just down a row. If the speaker looks at one person, then the person next to him, then the person next to her, all in a row, it gives a robot-like appearance.

If a speaker at an event has occasion to use a Teleprompter, there is another problem to consider: in these situations, the speaker's gaze may seem unfocused and even spacey, because facial expressions are naturally generated by looking at people, not inanimate objects. A secondary problem is when Teleprompters are positioned on each side of a room: audience members may begin to pay more attention to the predictable movement of the speaker's head from side to side (as if watching a tennis match), than what's being said. President Obama tends to exhibit this pattern when he speaks, and it's a wonder he hasn't been coached to do this differently.

In formal group settings, each time eye contact is established with an audience member, choose someone some distance away from the person previously chosen and be sure to change eye contact randomly. To facilitate this, when I present to a large group (say, 30 plus people), I mentally divide the audience into nine sections: three across and three deep and move my eye contact from one section to another which ensures coverage to everyone—those in the front, back, and sides of the room. This tactic works especially well in very large groups (say, 60 plus people), and is an indispensable tool. I talk to one person in a section, complete one thought (about five seconds), and pause while moving my eyes to a another person in a different section.

Even though I'm looking at only one individual at a time, the others around that person also feel like I'm looking individually at them because of the distance, so changing sections like this is important. It's also important to change sections without any perceptible pattern—no tennis match action, please! You want the audience to focus on your content, not your form.

Always change eye contact from one person to another during a natural pause in a sentence (where commas or periods would be), and take a breath as you move to each new person. A very short, one- or two-second pause gives audience members a chance to digest what they've heard. The brief silence, as you change eye contact, will feel like an eternity until it becomes a habit. Get used to it. It won't feel like an eternity to your audience. You'll look more confident and friendly, more knowledgeable. To see what I mean, watch polished speakers. Pauses are effective for listeners (the brief silence gives them a chance to absorb content), and they also help the speaker maintain an effective pace, so everybody wins. Speakers who don't make eye contact or use pauses are highly unlikely to be persuasive or viewed as credible.

To summarize, each eye contact with a listener should last long enough to complete a thought—five seconds or so—and include just one person at a time, whether it's a small group or a large group. If you miss any person (in a small group) or section (in a large group), people will feel left out—even though that feeling may only register subconsciously.

When only two people are interacting, it's equally important for both people to have good eye contact with each other. In this situation, the listener doesn't have the choice to gaze off into space without being noticed, and the speaker doesn't have the option to pause and move eye contact to someone new. Here's the solution: when speaking, look away periodically during a natural pause (as if, for example, you're thinking about the content of the discussion) to avoid giving that "stared-at" feeling. Slight head gestures will also help solve the problem.

Just as direct eye contact conveys interest and confidence, not looking at someone has the opposite effect. Speakers who talk to walls, ceilings, and floors will not look connected or confident. They will come across as unsure and uninteresting. Those who have a habit of bad eye contact probably don't know. If they did, they would definitely want to correct it. Some people's eye contact with humans is non-existent: one of my business colleagues talks only to the floor—hard to imagine he's unaware of this bad habit, but he must be, or he wouldn't do it. Because so many people are unskilled at good eye contact, it's essential to be choosy when you're deciding whom to ask for feedback. Most people will be "polite" and say your eye contact is fine. Polite babble, even if it comes with good intentions, isn't what you need in order to improve.

Eye movements, of course, communicate many other things. They can roll (indicating disagreement? frustration?), squint (indicating skepticism? lack of understanding?), widen (indicating surprise? fright?), close (not paying attention? sleeping?), glare (embarrassed? furious?), and so on. As an old Yiddish proverb says, *The eyes are the mirrors of the soul.* Be conscious of what your eyes are doing, and what they silently communicate. Good eye contact is required for good communication.

If you have any concerns about how to get credible feedback, find a workshop on public speaking (be choosy—not all of them are good), or invest in a personal coach for one-on-one attention (be choosy—not all of them are good). These professionals offer advice tailored to an individual's specific improvement areas and often use video recordings to help clients literally see that proper techniques increase credibility. It's well worth the time and money to seek this kind of help, so take advantage of the opportunity. Seeing the "effective you" on screen is invaluable—you'll feel extra motivated to break bad habits. Because so many people have ineffective eye contact, those who master it really stand out.

Main Points of Facial Expression and Eye Contact:
- Facial expressions are powerful communication tools.
- Don't assume how others are feeling by their facial expressions. To verify, ask them.
- When feelings are important, express them in words.
- Reinforce words with compatible facial expressions.
- Good eye contact helps speakers look confident.
- Lots of people have ineffective eye contact, so those who master it stand out.
- Eyes communicate unspoken messages.

Body Language. It's liberating to *feel* confident and relaxed in the presence of Clueless Emperors, but it's even more important to *look* confident and relaxed. With consistent practice, people with a polished appearance will actually begin to feel self-assured over time. How can that be? The positive feedback you'll get will confirm it: rigorous practice with new behaviors eventually creates new habits that replace the ineffective ones not serving your best interests. For example, if you feel nervous in front of a group, demonstrating effective behaviors (through facial expressions, eye contact, and body language) helps create a convincing appearance, even if you're a jumble of nerves on the inside. In short order, the new habits themselves will inspire confidence and eventually reduce anxiety.

What to do with legs, feet, arms, and hands? Specifics are coming up, but first some general information about body language. Never move your body in any way that gives an appearance of either aggression on one end of the scale or helplessness on the other end. Extremes are not useful. It's important to appear confident, controlled, and relaxed at all times, in every setting. As a testimonial, I recently saw a jazz concert where the female singer, Jessica Molaskey, used every body language skill recommended in this section, and she

looked great! Her physical presence added a lot to her performance.

Body movements are always on display (unless you are
truly alone), so don't think you can do what you want because
people won't notice. Assume they will. It's a wise person who
assumes there is always someone around who is observing and
evaluating. Even though it may be true that no one is watching,
why take the chance of doing something goofy that later
appears on YouTube as the laugh of the week?

What is your gait—lumbering, or confident? How are your
table manners—pushing food with fingers, or using utensils
properly? How is your posture—slumped or straight? People
send unintended messages in subtle ways that unnecessarily
hurt their credibility. There is nothing to lose by getting rid of
bad physical habits, and a lot to gain by adopting effective ones.

Legs and Feet. During any kind of verbal exchange,
whether it's to a group or just one individual, feet should be
positioned about hip-width distance apart with weight
balanced evenly on both legs. I've noticed this stance is more
often practiced by men.

Why don't women commonly stand with their weight
evenly balanced on both legs? My theory is that girls are social-
ized to use "feminine," almost ballet-like stances—as an
example, positioning one foot perpendicular to the other, heel
to arch. They're often advised to keep feet and legs close
together, whether seated or standing, so they look more "ladylike." Another girlish pose I've noticed recently in fashion
advertisements: models turn one foot inward like a pigeon toe,
and tilt the head to one side or looking down. Unfortunately,
this trend seems to be catching on—I see it everywhere in print
ads and am hoping it doesn't become a pose for young women
to imitate.

Our bodies weren't designed to bear our full weight on

one leg for long periods. Anyone standing in this "ladylike" pose tends to get uncomfortable over time, so she has to shift her weight back and forth to relieve pressure. When people do this, they look wobbly, weak, unsure, or helpless—so this behavior isn't going to inspire confidence, especially with Clueless Emperors. The goal is to look poised, confident, and relaxed—not feminine, fussy, or girlish.

In formal presentations, it's common to see presenters pace back and forth, non-stop. Please don't do this. A few steps now and again are fine, if you must. Relentless pacing is not fine. It may get rid of pent-up energy on the speaker's part, but it's very distracting to the audience. Remember that every physical move a speaker makes should support content—pacing doesn't meet that criteria. Podiums prevent the pacing problem, but avoid using one—it's more powerful to be out in the open, rather than hiding behind a block of wood.

In informal settings, we often have a choice to sit or stand during an interaction. Standing is usually perceived as a more aggressive choice (especially during a disagreement), while taking a seated position tends to ease tension. The best choice for the end goal is a judgment call. In my experience, diffusing tension is more likely to encourage open dialogue.

Avoid bouncing legs and tapping feet while seated. These movements are distracting to anyone who can see it. Also remember good posture. Slumped shoulders or a reclining posture may be interpreted as ill health, low self-esteem, or lack of interest. Sit up straight and stand up straight to avoid developing a permanently rounded back—and eventually lose the ability to pull back your shoulders altogether.

Arms and Hands. Unless you're gesturing, arms should hang gracefully along the sides of the body with hands and fingers slightly open, in a neutral position. Fidgeting is taboo. Listeners are distracted by unnecessary movement and will lose track of what the speaker is saying, while they watch what the speaker is doing. Crossing one's arms is acceptable, though it should be avoided in formal presentations. Crossed arms can be interpreted as either protective or aggressive—even if untrue—and shouldn't be a default position. Hands in pockets as a default position is also generally a no-no, unless you're an executive who wants to seem casual and approachable in front of the troops. Executives who do this, however, should follow through and actually be approachable in real life when they're off the stage. To do otherwise makes them come across as phony. Every physical movement should support content; otherwise, maintain a neutral position between gestures with arms at the sides of the body. This may be uncomfortable at first, but once it becomes a habit, it will feel like second nature. Always remember that movement without a purpose detracts from content.

When it's time for gestures (use lots of them), they should be fluid and provide an illustrative explanation of content. How tall is something? How wide? How important was it? Which way did someone go? Don't just tell us. Show us. If you're referring to something large, spread your arms wide. Don't worry, you won't take flight. Be descriptive. As an example, when talking about something that happens repeatedly, use a rolling motion with one arm. To emphasize that something is important, raise one arm (starting with the shoulder) to indicate its significance. Avoid repeated gestures and forearm-only gestures—they're too small and tend to look robotic. Practice large gestures, using one or both arms, starting at the shoulder, until it becomes comfortable. Frequent gestures (several in one sentence aren't too many, if they're descriptive and fluid) are recommended. They add power to physical presence and work well in both formal and informal settings.

Gesturing will feel uncomfortable during the practice

phase—if this behavior is new—not because it's ineffective. Think of gestures as a scaled-down version of charades—try playing a few games with friends or family to ease yourself into using them. It's a fun training exercise that increases comfort level.

If you've known people who have been mocked because of their gestures, it's probably because the gestures were too small, too programmed (think of old-fashioned orators who used standardized gestures for emphasis), not descriptive, or because they were repetitive instead of varied. Never use the same gesture over and over again. It's incredibly distracting.

A speaker appears weak if gestures are too small—elbows glued to the sides of the body coupled with flapping forearms contributes to a perception the speaker is fragile or unsure of content, to say nothing of the resemblance to a bird. Gestures made only from the wrists, with arms held rigidly at the sides of the body, is another look to completely avoid.

Ineffective gestures come in various forms: one of my clients used to lock arms at his sides (some well-meaning person gave him this dreadful advice years before), and he would nod his head for emphasis—several times per sentence. His energy had to go somewhere! Of course, this behavior made him look like a woodpecker, which was indeed a distraction. And to think no one had ever told him. He was completely unconscious of doing this until he attended a coaching seminar. When it was time to review his video   there were a few seconds of complete silence as he started watching—out came a great big laugh on himself. I'm quite sure he hasn't done any head-bobbing since that moment.

Physical movement attracts the eye, so gestures and stance should support content. In between gestures, arms should come gently down to rest along the sides of the body. I recently saw a video on the website of a $500M company—the Vice President of marketing was wringing her hands in seeming despair for three full minutes as she pitched the value of her company's products. Painful to watch and hard to believe. *Doesn't anybody review these things before they go public?*

Gestures can be as large as the space from the waist to above the head in height and a full arm's length away from the body in width, but not all gestures need to be that size, unless you're presenting to a large audience—people in the back rows will lose interest if gestures are small. Use one arm or both; just make sure gestures start at the shoulder with elbows away from the body, and keep gestures in the vicinity of the face. Listeners' eyes are drawn to movement, so keep their focus on one area.

It's important to develop a personal style, but those style decisions should make logical sense using the advice given here. Form should always support content. Frequent gestures open the body and convey confidence, so it's important to incorporate them into your form. The goal is to look confident, *not* programmed. Practice in front of a mirror or video camera. Watch people who do it well and copy them. Get training from a coach or member of a professional organization that specializes in public speaking. Most people don't know how to capitalize on form, so grab the opportunity to shine in this area.

Main Points of Body Language:
- When standing, legs should be about hip width apart.
- When standing, weight should be balanced on both legs.
- Gestures should generally be large (lead from the shoulder, not the forearm) and descriptive, not small and repetitive.

- Arms should remain at the sides of the body between gestures.
- Avoid pacing in formal presentations.
- Form should always support content.

Physical Appearance. Just as we judge a book by its cover—even though we're advised not to—people do judge us by how we look. Our physical appearance influences how people size us up, including how they assess trustworthiness, ability, and even intelligence. Think about what people see when they look at you, and how they might interpret what they see. It may seem unfair that physical appearance influences how others determine our value, but it's an unavoidable fact of life. Consider how you want to look in a given situation and plan ahead. Take advantage of whatever physical-appearance choices might enhance your presence, and therefore your credibility.

We can change our physical appearance in a number of ways; some are easy and others come with varying levels of difficulty. For the purposes of this section, I'll focus on the elements of appearance that can be modified without going to extreme measures. Anything related to gender, skin color, bone structure, physical features, height, and age is excluded. Many other aspects of physical appearance can be adjusted, and in some cases transformed.

Following are the modifiable elements that contribute to the total picture of a person's physical appearance. The suggestions that follow will improve the chances of getting neutral to favorable reviews by 8-out-of-10 people. The advice is given in the spirit of ensuring that your message, not your appearance, is the main event. Recommendations are for both genders unless otherwise specified. The broad categories addressed here are:

- Skin
- Teeth
- Body piercings and tattoos
- Hair
- Cleanliness
- Clothing
- Shoes
- Jewelry and other accessories
- Makeup
- Weight

Skin
- Keep your skin smooth and blemish-free. Products on the market can help with this—use them.
- Remember your hands. People sometimes forget how often their hands are front and center. Ragged cuticles and/or chewed nails are noticeable and distracting.
- For women, avoid nails that are long to an extreme, nail polish in unusual colors, or nail decorations.

Teeth
- Few of us are fortunate enough to have straight, white teeth by nature. If yours aren't, you may want to consider options for improving your smile. Your teeth are on display *every day*, so why not make them beautiful? Some procedures are expensive, but look at it this way: straight white teeth will never go out of style or be replaced by new technology. And you can amortize the cost over a lifetime.

Body Piercings and Tattoos
- Body piercings (other than pierced ears for women) and tattoos that aren't hidden by clothing have a limited

appreciative audience. If you're thinking about this fashion option, why take the chance on giving yourself a "permanent reminder of a temporary feeling," as a Jimmy Buffett song advises ("Permanent Reminder of a Temporary Feeling," from *Beach House on the Moon*). People won't negatively judge others because they don't have piercings or tattoos (gangs might be an exception), but they might negatively judge people who have them. If you insist on doing this, pick a location on your body that isn't visible when you're dressed. If it's too late, and you already have a "permanent reminder," there are painful and expensive ways of removing tattoos if you've discovered the harsh reality of bias against them.

Hair
- Facial hair where it doesn't belong is a no-no. The aging process isn't always kind, so if you're of an age where this is a concern, it's very easy to correct. Do it.
- If you're tempted to get a hairpiece, let the feeling pass—with few exceptions, it won't increase your credibility, and may harm it. For men especially, this is a major hair error.
- Keep hair trimmed and styled at a frequency that's right for your hair growth—in most cases every two to four months.
- Hair should look healthy. If you've abused yours, and there is nothing that can be done to correct it, cut it and start over.
- For men, don't even think about a comb-over or a dye job.
- For men, the choice to have a mustache or beard needs careful consideration. Sometimes beards work, and sometimes they don't, depending on your environment, and how your facial hair looks grown out. Scraggly, sparse,

and long just don't make the grade. If you do decide to grow one, keep it neat, short, and trimmed. And shave your neck.

- For women, if you color your hair, choose a shade that a person could actually have by nature (not, for example, deep purple, hot pink, or mahogany red) and is compatible with your coloring. It's best to have color done professionally unless you really, really know what you're doing. Any hair color that looks "done at home" should be turned over to a professional.

Cleanliness

- Everything about you should be clean. Your hair, skin, clothes, and shoes should all be immaculate. Clean never offends anyone, and as the saying goes, it's "next to godliness."

Clothing

- Styles and norms vary widely across cultures, geography, and industries. Do the homework to ensure you're properly attired for your surroundings.
- Make sure clothes fit well. If they're too big or too tight, they will draw attention. Also keep the setting in mind, and avoid being over-dressed or under-dressed for any occasion you attend. Don't stand out in a way that doesn't reflect your intentions, but serves your best interests instead. A pulled-together look keeps the focus on what you have to say, not how you look.
- Never wear pants so small they can't fit across your waistline, and consequently ride below an overhanging belly.
- For women, sexy clothing is fine in social settings, but keep in mind that sexy and tacky are not the same thing: showing too much skin, especially at work or social

functions connected with work, communicates low self-esteem. Eye-catching, yes. Classy, no.
- Rumpled clothes will generally be taken less seriously than clothes that are neat and pressed.

Shoes
- Shoes should be appropriate for the setting—as an example, no sneakers at important meetings unless everyone else has them on—and make sure whatever you're wearing isn't scuffed or worn-out looking. Wear current styles without buying anything so fashionable that you're one of the first to show them off in public.
- For women, sky-high heels make walking gracefully a challenge. If you wear them, make sure you can walk in them without looking goofy.

Jewelry and other Accessories
- Keep it simple. Multiple rings, earrings, necklaces, or bracelets are distracting.
- If you wear glasses, choose a current style with a size and shape appropriate for your face.
- Briefcases and handbags should be compatible with your environment. Avoid anything along the lines of flashy, floppy, flamboyant, or flowered. If you don't know what "appropriate" looks like, observe people who look polished and copy the look, or ask a trusted advisor for tips.

Makeup
- The good news is that appropriate choices vary widely other than avoiding a heavy or overdone look. The best advice is to fit in wherever you are, unless being unique and standing out is your objective.

Weight

• One of the toughest appearance problems to fix, of course, is weight reduction if you're overweight. Anyone who struggles with maintaining a healthy weight knows how hard it is to stay fit. We all know the positive results of healthy eating and adequate exercise—good physical shape improves the quality and length of life. But, like it or not, weight also makes a difference in how we're perceived. And a fit body will never go out of style or be inappropriate. Rising obesity statistics are not going to change the negative bias that overweight people experience. If keeping fit has been a problem for you in the past, I hope you can conquer it to improve your future. Use your willpower and all the resources available to get healthy and look great.

As you can see, the overarching goal regarding appearance is to fit in and avoid drawing attention to appearance. It's your content that should stand out above all else. How you look should never be so noticeable that it gets people talking—in a negative way. Somewhat different is acceptable, stunningly unique is not, with one exception: if you happen to be especially good-looking, count your blessings.

When appearance takes center stage, credibility suffers—be mindful of the choices you make, so your content is the main event. Consider the example of performers. Madonna, Elton John, and Lady Gaga use costuming to create a persona. But it's risky to imitate a rock star without understanding how you'll be perceived and reviewed by family members, friends, peers, business associates, or Clueless Emperors. However you choose to present yourself is fine, so long as you fit in with the majority of people in the environment. When it comes to appearance, it's all about physically "disappearing" in the crowd if you want to be credible.

Ample, easy-to-find resources give additional information and detail about specific questions you may have about physical appearance. Be sure to check them out if you're not sure which choices are best for your lifestyle.

> ### Main Points of Physical Appearance:
> - How you look communicates a message of its own.
> - Many elements contribute to a person's physical appearance—and they all require attention.
> - Be deliberate about the image you create.
> - Content and presence, not physical appearance, should be the main event.
> - If your physical appearance separates you from acceptable norms, expect negative biases.

Physical Timing. We learned about auditory timing in the previous chapter. Physical timing is also a powerful communication behavior. Most people don't think strategically about physical timing, but those who give it consideration have a better shot at overcoming Clueless Emperors. Why is this so? Because "good timing" means choosing the precise moment to do something for optimum effect. Physical timing includes the choices people make when they (A) show up physically and (B) make any kind of body movement:

A) *Showing up physically* refers to when you decide to make an appearance, and whether that appearance is early, on time, or late. Examples of this are the time of day you meet a friend to see a movie, attend a meeting, stop by a colleague's office with a question, or arrive at an appointment. When do you show up? People get reputations regarding their timeliness. Are you generally early, on time, or late? A friend of mine is self-aware enough to know that left to his own devices, he's usually fifteen minutes late for everything. He compensates for this innate lack of timeliness by setting his watch fifteen minutes fast and says this tactic helps. It's a practical solution for him.

Running late is also a natural tendency of mine—but I realize that showing up late is rude, so it's a demon worth battling. Most people, of course, don't appreciate tardiness in others. Being on time is understandably interpreted as thoughtful citizenship, so I work conscientiously to be on time. But setting my watch fifteen minutes ahead doesn't work for me—I would always know in the back of my mind that the time on my watch wasn't real. My little strategy is to always plan for an early arrival, which usually gets me where I want to be just on time. Invent your own method to stay on schedule if you have a problem with timeliness.

If no one is expecting you, let your timing demon run amok. Running behind schedule is fine when no one is inconvenienced—and you feel calm and collected no matter what may or may not get checked off your to-do list. However, if running late makes you internally frantic, even when no one is counting on you, the stress isn't worth it.

If you have a bad habit of being late much of the time, it's likely you're regularly annoying others. Isn't it frustrating that airplanes just won't wait when we're behind schedule? It's fair to expect that anyone who makes a commitment to show up at a specific time should actually be there at that time. That said, if those who are timely don't like waiting for latecomers—who does?—feedback may be in order. Being late *always* requires an apology to those who have waited, and perpetual lateness needs to be reformed. If being on time is a problem, fixing it is a fabulous idea, so people don't have to be disappointed that you've arrived late—again.

Another potential timing problem occurs when we initiate a conversation on the fly, either through a phone call or stopping by for a face-to-face interaction. At such times, we are, in effect, interrupting. In these circumstances, it's thoughtful to ask, "Is this a good time to talk?" unless it's a one-minute discussion item. An argument could be made that if someone answers the phone, they're implicitly agreeing to an interruption, but asking whether it's a convenient time to talk is usually appreciated. If you stop by in person, it's a requirement to ask this question to ensure the person whose attention you want is truly available to listen to what you have to say. People you "need" to talk to aren't twiddling their thumbs, waiting for you and your burning issue to appear at their doorstep.

Procrastination is another element of physical timing. Sometimes it's hard to get up in the morning; sometimes we just don't feel motivated to start an activity or a project—right now. Procrastinators have different ways of approaching tasks and commitments. Sometimes they rush around at the last minute; other times they delay to the point of missing the deadline. If habitual procrastination has caused you difficulty in the past, eliminating the unnecessary stress it causes, for you and others, is an improvement opportunity.

B) *Body movements* draw attention—raising an arm, taking a step forward or back, shaking hands, and turning around are examples. Body movements are not always similarly interpreted by those who see them. For instance, nodding one's head (indicating agreement? or acknowledgement?), shaking one's head (indicating disagreement? or disbelief?), squinting the eyes (indicating skepticism? or lack of trust?), and a quick intake of breath (indicating shock? or delight?) can be perceived many different ways. In other words, physical movement often communicates a message of its own—with no guarantees of how that movement will be interpreted.

Body movements are usually executed while we're on

autopilot and generally don't create problems. As with most generalizations, however, there are exceptions. As an example, imagine a crowded movie theater or concert hall where someone has to finagle his way across people in their seats in order to make an exit. Doing this once may be forgiven, but anything more than that will certainly be annoying to those who are inconvenienced. Late-comers also qualify in this situation.

Sometimes even slight body movements send not-so-subtle messages. Slightly nodding one's head while someone is talking is an example. This movement will probably come across as agreeing with what's being said, whether or not that's the intention.

Be conscious of how and when you move, because if it happens at the wrong time, people might be distracted. Ever been around someone tapping a pencil, cracking knuckles, jiggling a leg, chomping gum, talking with a hand covering the mouth, or showing bad table manners? Any repetitive, mindless movement diverts people's attention. It's like a calling card to Clueless Emperors that says, "I don't have self-control, so do with me what you will."

The timing of *written* communication (letter, e-mail, or handwritten note) is also worth special mention. How to decide when the timing is right? As an example, promptly written thank-you notes or e-mail responses send a positive signal. E-mail etiquette has evolved into a sub-culture with specific expectations. Your dependability may be questioned if you delay sending the messages on your to-do list.

Some people appreciate reminder notes—if written in a respectful tone. I love them. If you love them, let the people in your life know, but don't assume everyone feels the same. Check it out before you return the favor.

Main Points of Physical Timing:
- Showing up early or on time for meetings or gatherings demonstrates commitment.
- Any physical movement sends a message of its own and is distinct from the content of the message.
- Actions related to goals or projects should be completed in a time frame that meets or exceeds commitments.

The Setting. Most often, the setting where a communication takes place doesn't carry special significance. If there is an emotional element to the message, however, it becomes important to consider the setting. When you're able to control or influence where a communication takes place, take advantage of the opportunity and think about the emotional side of what needs to be said when choosing a location. The choice may influence whether there is a successful result. The following situations show how an appropriate setting could influence the outcome of a transaction:

- Talking with your child about inappropriate behavior that needs correction
- Giving developmental feedback to a poor-performing employee
- Delivering important information to your boss
- Giving feedback to a friend about something serious or personal

The importance of deliberately selecting the setting for a discussion is directly related to the level of emotion involved in the content. Emotionally charged issues require an especially thoughtful approach. Clueless Emperors lack emotional skills, so to succeed with them, you'll need to manage the setting whenever possible. Assuming you're able to influence where a meeting or conversation will take place, consider the following:

- By phone or face-face?
- Whose office?
- Whose home?
- Noisy or quiet surroundings?
- In public or in private?
- In a neutral location or one that may be familiar to either party?

The purpose of the communication provides clues for choosing the best setting. Is it instructional? Are you giving a directive, delivering feedback, praising, or expressing disappointment about something? One way to select a positive setting that's conducive to the message is to think about where *you* would want to meet if you were receiving the message you plan to deliver.

Main Points of Setting:
- The purpose of a communication should influence the setting.
- The emotional element of a message should influence the setting.
- Use whatever influence you have to choose where a communication takes place.

Word Choice When Writing. Choosing the words for a written message is one of the most important and complex communication decisions we make. This section focuses on written word choice, but most of the advice also applies to the spoken word discussed in the previous chapter. First, let's differentiate between the content of a message and word choices. Only the writer knows the particular content she wishes to convey, and this book is not intended to help with content. Subject matter can be written in several acceptable ways using various words with similar meanings. Although it's possible to maintain the basic substance of a message with any number of words and sentence constructions, changing words can also significantly change the tone and nuance of what is communicated. Choosing the right words at the right time is a crucial skill—and it's challenging to master. There are many ways to write effectively, but there are just as many ways to butcher communication and get into trouble.

Tone plays a significant role in writing and speaking, because it goes beyond content and infuses a message with whatever emotions are linked to that content, all without communicating it directly. Each of the following pairs of statements conveys the same basic content. However, there is a substantial difference in tone because of the words that are chosen to convey that content. In each case, B is generally interpreted to have a more civilized and respectful tone:

A. I can't go to that meeting—I have too much work to do.
B. I won't be able to attend the meeting today, but tomorrow afternoon would work.

A. Would you please return my call?
B. I know you've been busy. Please call when you get a chance.

A. Why didn't you do what I asked?
B. I'm wondering how we misunderstood each other.

A. Please be on time tomorrow.

B. I would really appreciate it if you could arrive at three o'clock tomorrow.

A. I don't want to go out.
B. I'd love to go out tonight, but I'm exhausted and need a full night's sleep.

Using a respectful tone (as shown in the B examples above) is considered by 8-out-of-10 people to be a more Clued-In approach. Nevertheless, there are times when escalation and directness are in order, so a stronger tone could be a legitimate choice. Only the sender knows what level of emotion and directness is required in a particular circumstance. Your choices will affect how you're viewed by people who receive your communication. Habits that contribute to gaining a reputation—being "quick on the draw" or "hard to read" are examples—should be avoided.

If you've developed word-choice habits, written or spoken, that others have come to *expect*—whether they're more like A or B above, or some other tone—you've missed the opportunity word choices offer. In other words, it's important to draw on a variety of moods depending on the emotion you wish to weave into your content—don't be predictable. The point of comparing the statements in the previous examples—and understanding the difference—is to show the power of word choice and tone.

The words we use should be well thought out, not a gut response. Choose your words deliberately and with care. Become known for good writing, not for having a predictable, dominant style. If you want to become more aware of how people "hear" you, ask for feedback from skilled friends and colleagues, or a professional coach.

The ability to select just the right words will get your

messages across in just the right way, but it's going to take some work if word mastery is not one of your current strengths. The English language is complicated. If you decide to improve your vocabulary, or your ability to put words together for maximum effect, it might initially feel like an overwhelming task. Take comfort that expertise will develop over time, and the effort will have a huge payoff. Crafting the right tone is an art form that will favorably serve you for a lifetime—words are here to stay as communication devices for the foreseeable future.

The advantage of the written word over the spoken word is that we have time—usually in private—to edit and revise a message before sending it. If a particular communication is especially important, it's a good idea to ask someone you trust to review the document, and remember not to think, or act, like a Clueless Emperor when you get the feedback.

If you have doubts whether learning how to choose the right words and tone (written or spoken) is worth the effort, pay close attention to the way people respond to you for one month. It's not difficult to understand how people feel if we take note of their non-verbal communication.

How we write leaves an impression with readers. The time it takes to undo a message that riles people up isn't worth it: review and edit e-mails *before* clicking the send button. Using appropriate words makes intent clear. It also reduces misunderstandings and saves time in the long run. Consider saving a month's worth of e-mails, then with the benefit of hindsight, review and assess whether different words would have improved the content.

Although the world of words presents complicated and varied challenges, a common bad habit is the use of "I" versus "you" in certain circumstances. Consider the pairs of statements in the following examples (which apply to both writing and speaking):

A. You missed my point.
B. I don't think I said that clearly.

A. You hurt my feelings.
B. I feel hurt.

A. You made me late for work.
B. I was late for work.

These examples show that using "I" instead of an accusatory "you" conveys personal accountability and will likely reduce a receiver's defensiveness.

Main Points of Word Choice in Writing:
- Be aware that words have shades of meaning. It's important to choose words that precisely convey what's intended.
- Ask for feedback before sending important written messages.
- Take the time to review, edit, and correct written work.
- Make a habit of using "I" instead of "you" where appropriate, especially when giving feedback.

Punctuation. In written messages, punctuation helps readers better understand the content. Punctuation can indicate emphasis (exclamation points, italics, or upper-case letters), a pause (commas, em dashes, colons, semicolons, or periods), ownership (apostrophes), tone (question marks, exclamation points, boldface, or italics), and so on. Many an e-mail has ruffled feathers, or worse, because the writer used incorrect, ineffective, or inappropriate punctuation. As an example, using all capital letters looks—and in our heads, sounds—like YELLING. Incorrect punctuation can ruin a message. If your punctuation comes off as abrupt, you will be viewed as an abrupt person.

Many resources are available to improve punctuation: *The Elements of Style* by Strunk and White, Fourth Edition (Allyn & Bacon, 2000), *Eats, Shoots & Leaves* by Lynne Truss (Gotham Books, 2003), and *Grammar Girl's Quick and Dirty Tips for Better Writing* by Mignon Fogarty (Henry Holt and Company, LLC, 2008) are three good options.

Main Points of Punctuation:
• We show inflection in written work through punctuation.
• Punctuation adds meaning to the content of a message.

Length of a Written Message. How do we decide how long or short a written message or document should be? Situations vary, so there aren't any specific rules to answer this question. In school, teachers usually assign the length of a paper, but we seldom receive such guidance at work. Legal briefs are limited to a specific length—even judges have a threshold—and e-mails and office documents are usually appreciated when they're short. People just won't read memos or reports that are seemingly endless.

Generally, the shorter the message the better, especially with e-mails or documentation of work activities. When written messages are concise and clear, readers are able to get through them quickly ... and they will love the writer for keeping it simple. Long, rambling epistles may be easier for the writer (no editing time required), but they are hard on the reader. Pascal was right when he said, "I have made this letter longer than usual, because I lack the time to make it short." And as William S. Strunk and E.B. White say so succinctly in *The Elements of Style*, "Omit needless words," so I will do that now.

Main Points of Length of a Written Message:
• Try to keep written messages short unless you're writing a book.
• Short messages are reader-friendly.

The Visible Bottom Line

So there you have it—a detailed description of the visible skills that can be used to engage Clued-In citizens and overcome Clueless Emperors. There are many capabilities to keep in mind, and they all contribute to effective communication. To avoid feeling overwhelmed, assess what you need to work on and practice new skills one at a time. None of the skills are difficult in and of themselves, but it does take concentration and discipline to break bad habits and use the skills simultaneously.

A metaphor to illustrate how we make judgments based on what we see is to compare people's skills to the threads in a piece of fabric. If some threads have unraveled, the fabric is weaker. Any snags are obvious. If the color has faded, the piece of fabric looks worn out. Any buyer looking at cloth that's damaged will pass it by. It might still be usable, but it looks tattered and sloppy. It's not as attractive as when it was intact. When all the threads are in good condition and in their proper place, the fabric is more pleasing to the eye and gets noticed, while the less attractive cloth gets ignored.

This is what happens when the total package of visible communication skills has been mastered. We might be good at word choices, but if we have a sloppy physical appearance, we undermine our credibility. We might be great with facial expressions, but our poor posture makes us look weak and timid. We might be great at punctuation, but write such long e-mails that our receivers feel overwhelmed and hit the delete button, or set our messages aside until they can gather strength to plow through them. Any thread that is frayed or missing from the fabric of visible skills diminishes our potential to be convincing and persuasive.

"Did I really behave that way? What was I thinking?"
—A Recovering Clueless Emperor

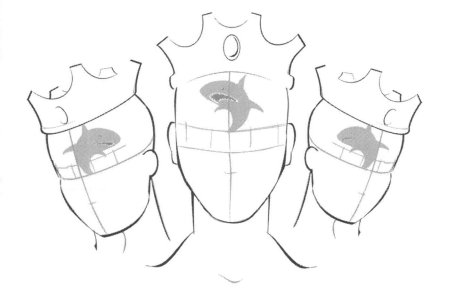

PART IV

Implementing
the Skills

CHAPTER 16

Integrating New Behavior into Your Life

"Practice is the best of all instructors."
—Publilius Syrus

This chapter presents some brief, real-life cases starring Clueless Emperors—in a variety of home and work situations—that will help you visualize how the physical skills (in Chapters 14 and 15) work together. At the end of each case, there is a suggested strategy for what the Clueless Emperor's target might do to solve the stated problem. There is always more than one way to overcome a Clueless Emperor, so I invite you to create solutions of your own after reading the cases. Just be sure to incorporate the skills described in this book. You'll see how well they work.

Any strategy to overcome a Clueless Emperor has two elements: the plan itself (content) and the physical skills (form) to implement that plan. This book was written to help you improve your form, or *how* you're going to implement the content in your head. The audible and visible physical skills detailed in the previous chapters will help you do this. Content is always situation specific and unique, but the skills associated with great form are relatively universal.

In each of the following cases, I reference *content* (the part your intellect is responsible for) where it's applicable, and the *specific behaviors* (the part your voice and body are responsible for) where they are applicable to help you differentiate between the two.

The last case in this chapter is a situation where neither of the characters has official power, and each of them has the potential to be a target of the other. In this case, there is a strategy for each party.

Clueless Emperor Case #1

Brenda has been an administrative assistant for one year and reports to George, a director at the We-Communicate Company. She is competent at her job, but always strives to improve her skills. Her previous boss was good at giving developmental feedback, and as a result, Brenda was able to improve her job performance. But George has never given Brenda any feedback. Her annual appraisal is scheduled for Friday morning at ten o'clock, and she's looking forward to finding out how George evaluates her work.

On the day and time of Brenda's appraisal discussion, George is nowhere to be found. Brenda saw him first thing that morning, but hasn't seen him since then. When George finally shows up at 10:45 and walks right by Brenda saying nothing, she decides to be patient, thinking he'll call her shortly. That doesn't happen. After fifteen minutes, Brenda walks the few steps to George's office and asks if he'll be ready soon for their discussion. George looks agitated, says he totally forgot, and asks her to come in. She sits down across from his desk and listens as he explains that the evaluation form isn't quite finished yet. He says, in a hurried pace, that she's doing a great job, that he enjoys working with her, so he's giving her the second highest available rating—*Exceeds Expectations*—and says this as though the rating is a gift from heaven. George thanks her for stopping by, and without another word, turns his chair around and starts working on his e-mail.

Brenda is understandably upset. The so-called perform-ance review took less than two minutes. If George had given her the highest possible rating—*Far Exceeds*—she would undoubtedly have accepted it and kept any questions to herself, even though not getting developmental feedback would have been disappointing. This circumstance is frustrating, however, because Brenda thinks the highest rating is what she earned— and George has given her no feedback to substantiate the lower rating he did give her. She has no idea what *Far Exceeds* stan-dards are from his perspective, and was dismissed with no opportunity to ask questions or give feedback of her own. What can Brenda do to get a solid understanding of her current performance and get feedback for improvement?

Strategy for Brenda: When Brenda goes to George's office to ask if he's ready and he acknowledges he forgot their appointment, Brenda capitalizes on her awareness of George's personality and tells him the review is important to her (*Content*). She asks if he would prefer to reschedule (*Timing* and *Setting*) when he has less on his mind (*Word Choice*). Assuming George remains clueless about his responsibility as a manager and goes ahead with the appraisal meeting, Brenda knows she has no other choice than to agree. She doesn't hesi-tate (*Timing*) when George finishes his two-minute "review." She says she's confused (*Word Choice*) and asks (*Question*) how he determined the rating he gave her. She is careful to use a tone that indicates curiosity (*Volume* and *Inflection*) without indicating the frustration she actually feels (*Awareness*). He probably doesn't have the hard data to answer her question— she anticipates he won't be able to give her the information she wants (*Content*)—but she needs to get her question on the record (*Timing*). She knows her boss isn't emotionally intelli-gent, yet at the same time, she wants to get her needs met. Overhauling George's leadership style isn't on her to-do list.

Brenda tells George she would appreciate (*Word Choice*) feedback on her past year's performance, as well as discuss his expectations of her in the coming year (*Content*). She asks (*Question*) for a second meeting when he is less busy (*Timing* and *Word Choice*), allowing George to save face. In that future meeting, Brenda will have to take the lead and informally coach George about the difference between behaviors and perceptions, so she can get the kind of quality feedback she needs to improve. It's entirely possible that if Brenda suggests writing her own objectives and evaluation (*Content*), George will agree—his behavior indicates he doesn't want to do it himself. This task will add to Brenda's workload, but it will give her more control.

Clueless Emperor Case #2

Dad is grocery shopping with Angela, his five-year-old daughter. He's had a long day and is looking forward to getting the food shopping out of the way and enjoying a relaxing evening at home. As they pass through the candy aisle, Angela abruptly announces she wants some candy, and she wants it now! When Dad says no, Angela suddenly launches a kicking and screaming tantrum. Dad is embarrassed by the outburst, especially in light of the public setting. As other shoppers pretend not to stare, he tries to calm his child, all to no avail.

In this circumstance, Angela has situation power over her father. She may have learned that sobbing and yelling in public get her what she wants, but whether she's truly out of control or acting out on purpose, Dad still has an immediate problem. He wants to teach Angela that her behavior is not acceptable, but he struggles with how to do this in a public place. If she was having the tantrum at home, he could give her a time-out and let Angela carry on until she wore herself out. He considers turning around and going home to do just that, but he also wants to get the shopping done without caving in to Angela's fit.

People might assume parents have more power and control than a young child does, but this isn't always the case. Angela's situation power may evoke some parenting nightmares of your own. If a child has learned that bad behavior leads to winning, it's time to unspoil the child. As children get older, they find many more opportunities to behave like Clueless Emperors, so the stakes just get higher. Angela's fling with situation power is quite real. She is old enough to know a strategically executed temper tantrum might cause her father to fold. How can Dad do the right thing by Angela and also get the shopping done?

Strategy for Dad: An argument could be made that perhaps Dad is a Clueless Emperor himself if Angela behaves this way often because she's been allowed to get away with it on other occasions. We'll assume in this case that Angela has been busy learning bad behavior from a few delinquent nursery-school playmates and is surprising Dad with a fit of temper he isn't remotely expecting.

One choice for Dad is to carry on with the shopping and ignore Angela's tantrum, hoping it will go away (*Content*). But he's unwilling to do that. He wants to teach his daughter to behave appropriately in public and is willing to make some minor personal sacrifices in the process (*Content*). Dad doesn't want to go home without finishing the shopping (*Timing*), so he takes Angela out to the car (*Setting*). In a calm manner (*Awareness*), he gets her into the car seat, buckles her in, and says in a quiet tone (*Inflection* and *Volume*) that they will go back into the store when she feels better (*Word Choice*). He asks if she understands (*Question*), looks at her (*Eye Contact*), waits quietly (*Silence*) until she answers (*Timing*), then sits in the driver's seat and reads the newspaper (*Silence*). He pays no attention to her until the sobs begin to subside. At that point,

Dad asks Angela if she wants to go back inside the store, but this time without fussing (*Question*). He looks directly at her (*Eye Contact*), waits for an answer (*Silence* and *Timing*), and is careful not to over-talk (*Air Time*). If she agrees, they go back in the store to finish shopping. If Angela says "no," Dad will have to go back to reading in silence and wait her out, or forget the shopping and go home.

Generally speaking, the challenges of child rearing are beyond the scope of this book, except when children act like Clueless Emperors only upon occasion. If your child acts this way a lot of the time, you have a different predicament than can be solved in these pages. The strategy suggested here isn't intended to be a cure-all for juvenile tantrums—it's just one possible way to approach this sort of issue. In the long run, parents need to address these situations without being Clueless Emperors themselves. For starters, they should examine their past behaviors and consider whether, or how, they may have contributed to the problem. In this case, if Dad has occasionally given in to Angela's fits in the past, rather than consistently not doing so, he can expect more tantrums.

Clueless Emperor Case #3

Cindy is the CEO of a large company, Take-Charge, Inc. Her job gives her a lot of position power which she enjoys immensely. She has been traveling all week, working long hours in hotels and regional offices and is eager to get home. The corporate jet wasn't available for this trip, so Cindy is flying commercial. Because she has mega-frequent-flyer status, an upgrade is on her radar screen—it looks like a full flight, and she doesn't want to be stuck in coach class, where it will be crowded and noisy.

Cindy consistently takes full advantage of her CEO position and is used to having the last word on all matters. Aiming at enhancing her upgrade chances, therefore, she employs her customary command and control style with Larry, the gate agent. Speaking in a loud and authoritative voice, she makes sure he knows that she's a CEO and mega-frequent-flyer all rolled into one very important person. She tells him she's expecting an upgrade, and gives Larry no real opportunity to respond. It makes no sense for Cindy to annoy the one person who could potentially give her what she wants—Larry's situation power trumps Cindy's position power—but the Clueless Emperor in her brain is in full control. In this situation, Cindy has less power than she's used to, but that hasn't been taken into consideration. Certainly her rude performance at the gate indicates she doesn't have a clue.

First class has checked in full, so there is actually nothing Larry can do for Cindy. Although he is sort of privately pleased about that, he realizes Cindy may escalate her demand depending on how he gives her this information—and he'd like to keep that from happening. There are several mega-frequent-flyers on this flight, and Larry wants to keep them all happy—even Cindy—regardless of their upgrade status. How can he deliver appropriate customer service and protect himself against a tirade?

Strategy for Larry: Even though there isn't anything Larry can do to get Cindy into first class, were he so inclined, he's customer-focused and savvy enough to know that treating her with any level of disregard won't help with customer relations (*Awareness*)—though it's tempting. He's aware that he need not be clueless himself and chooses to use his situation power wisely instead. More pragmatically, he doesn't want Cindy to make a nonsense complaint that will take time to investigate (*Content*), and he knows that any visible frustration on his part gives her an incentive to do just that (*Awareness*). So Larry looks directly at her (*Eye Contact*) and nods his head (*Body*

Language) as she's talking, calmly waiting out her monologue (*Silence* and *Facial Expression*). When she's finished, he uses a sympathetic tone (*Inflection*) and says it seems like she's had a long week (*Word Choice* and *Timing*). He then quietly says (*Volume*), while giving her a comforting smile (*Facial Expression*), that he wishes (*Word Choice*) an upgrade were available, but first class is full—all passengers have checked in. He asks her (*Question*) if she would like coupons for a movie and beverage to help make the flight go by a little faster. Of course, Cindy isn't appeased by Larry's sympathy, but his behavior has taken the fight out of her. She finds it difficult to sustain her anger because Larry has shrewdly played to her ego and treated her with warmth. She realizes that asking to speak to a supervisor is useless, because Larry has given her no ammunition to escalate her frustration.

Clueless Emperor Case #4

Gloria's father, Dan, has come to visit and will be staying for one week. She's happy to have him as a guest—she enjoys his company and looks forward to their annual week together. He's a great dad and a skilled handyman who gets pleasure from helping her with the chores around the house that she can't do herself. One of their rituals is the to-do list that is always waiting for him when he arrives. All goes well with the visit. They enjoy a mix of relaxation and work, and Dan puts a huge dent in Gloria's list. One morning in the middle of his stay, he decides to go out and play a game of tennis while Gloria is out running errands. She returns home before her father and is surprised to see the garage door wide open, then discovers that the door going into the house from the garage is unlocked.

Gloria knows her father didn't purposefully leave the house unprotected, but she lives in the city and has told him several times that locking the doors is important. She feels it's reasonable to expect him to do this if he leaves the house when she's not there. At the same time, she's uncomfortable talking with her father about the problem. She knows it was nothing more than thoughtless on his part, but his need-to-be-right complex is mighty. Gathering fortitude—she believes it's better to be safe than sorry—when Dan comes home, she asks about not locking the doors.

"Well," he retorts defensively, "no one broke in, did they?"

Gloria has mixed feelings at this point. She loves her father and doesn't want to fight with him. She knows he grew up in a farm town where locking doors wasn't a choice—doors didn't have locks. At the same time she knows her dad is well aware that houses in the city require security, and that locking doors matters to her. If Dan acknowledges this, however, he can't be "right" about what he did.

Where does this leave Gloria? Is the situation a trivial matter that should be left alone? If this circumstance involved someone she would never see again, it would be the most sensible thing to do. Her frustration stems from the belief that her father could very well do the same thing again. She wants to avoid hurting his feelings, but also wants assurance the doors are locked. The approach she takes with him is important—preventing an argument is her goal. When this kind of Clueless Emperor behavior occurs frequently in family units, those who bear the brunt of defensive responses get hurt and build resentment over time. Learning how to stop this cycle can be a major stress reducer. How can Gloria avoid getting grudging compliance from her dad and get loving commitment instead?

Strategy for Gloria: When Dan gives Gloria a defensive response ("no one broke in, did they?"), she remains calm (*Facial Expression* and *Volume*) and asks (*Question*) how he would feel if someone *had* broken in (*Content*). She waits quietly for his answer (*Silence*). Dan will have to acknowledge a break-in would have been a bad thing. Gloria gently (*Inflection*) asks (*Question*) if he remembers how important it is to her that doors are locked when no one is home, and waits for his answer (*Silence* and *Timing*). Dan will probably say he remembers her request, because of the non-confrontational way (*Awareness*) she poses the question. Gloria then asks him "as a favor" (*Word Choice*) to her, to please lock doors when he is the last to leave the house. Stated this way, it's less likely Dan will be defensive because Gloria's approach will help him save face and reduce his need to defend. It's more likely he'll remember to lock the doors the next time he leaves the house.

Clueless Emperor Case #5

Frank is ready for a Saturday morning hike, but decides to do a quick scan of his work e-mail before heading out the door. One of the messages is a shocker—Jack, his usually mild-mannered boss with whom he has a cordial and open relationship, accuses Frank of being unprofessional on a recent project. Jack's tone is completely out of character. Frank reads the angry and derogatory words in the message, but can hardly believe his boss wrote them. It's clear that Jack is riled up over incorrect information he's received from some unknown person, and believes the story.

Feeling overwhelmed, Frank reads the e-mail again. At the end of the message, he notes that Jack actually acknowledges his information has come secondhand. Frank sees this as a light at the end of the tunnel. Although the last sentence in Jack's e-mail says, "I can only hope there's another side to the story," the words seem more rhetorical than sincere. Frank is especially concerned, because he has never experienced his boss showing this kind of hostility. How can Frank convince Jack that the information he received is incorrect?

Strategy for Frank: Frank knows his emotional response to Jack's anger needs to be managed. Defensiveness, or any expression of indignation on his part, would be unproductive (*Awareness*). He doesn't feel comfortable (*Emotion*) waiting until Monday to answer Jack's message, so he decides to delay his hike and respond right away (*Timing*). He knows the information Jack received isn't accurate (*Content*), so he wants his reply to be in writing—the facts will then be on record (*Choosing to Write His Message*). His goal is to clear up Jack's misconceptions (*Content*). Frank keeps the message short (*Length of a Written Message*), makes it easy to read (*Punctuation*), and writes clearly (*Word Choices*). When Frank completes a draft of his response to Jack, he sends it to Ken, a trustworthy colleague with good writing skills (*Word Choices* and *Punctuation*) to ensure the tone of his message is appropriate. After Ken makes some suggestions, Frank edits the message, then e-mails his reply to Jack. By addressing the issue immediately (*Timing*), Frank feels comfortable he's provided his boss with the facts he needs to fully understand the problem, and has given him ample time to decompress and think through the issue over the weekend (*Awareness* and *Timing*) before discussing it on Monday.

Clueless Emperor Case #6

Rick wakes up one morning with a sharp stomach pain that hasn't eased much by mid-day. He's concerned and calls to schedule an appointment with a specialist recommended by a friend. The receptionist, Erin, curtly offers an appointment date one month out. But Rick is worried about his symptoms. He certainly doesn't want to wait until the situation requires an emergency room visit, and would also prefer not making multiple phone calls to find another doctor who can see him sooner. When he asks if there is an earlier appointment, Erin says in a snappish tone that nothing is available. She doesn't acknowledge Rick's concern in any way. He believes if Erin knew him personally or was in a better mood, she would make an exception and schedule something sooner, but right now she is Rick's Clueless Emperor. His job is to persuade her to give him an appointment in the very near future. How can Rick avoid the hassle of making more phone calls and convince Erin to help him?

Strategy for Rick: Rick considers telling Erin he suspects there is something she could do, but his understanding of the need-to-be-right mentality (*Awareness*) indicates this argument may further entrench her in the position she's taken. He decides to show vulnerability instead and tells Erin that he's really worried (*Emotion*) about what the sudden pain means. He verbally acknowledges Erin's predicament (*Awareness*) and keeps his comments brief (*Air Time*). He pauses (*Silence*) to make sure she understands his worry is sincere, rather than over-talk (*Air Time*). His silence alone may prompt her to help him. If not, he can say he would prefer to go to this particular doctor, but because he needs to see a doctor soon, could Erin recommend someone else (*Question*)? If he's convincing (*Inflection* and *Word Choice*), and Erin believes he is sufficiently worried—and ready to take his money elsewhere—it's more likely she'll find an earlier appointment for him.

Clueless Emperor Case #7

Jenny has recently joined Walk-On-Tippie-Toes, Inc. and works for Ralph, CEO of the company. Ralph is famous for his charisma and infamous for his temper. His subordinates love him when he's in a friendly frame of mind, and maintain their distance when he loses his cool. The tension created by Ralph's unpredictable mood swings keeps people in the organization on high alert. As a new employee in the company, Jenny has not yet experienced his bad behavior, but she has heard the stories.

One day Ralph, in high-charisma mode, calls Jenny to his office and asks her to prepare a report that will serve as a basis for discussion in a meeting he's scheduling for the following morning. The topic is in Jenny's area of responsibility. Ralph is warm and friendly as he encourages her to take the lead in the meeting the next day. He says that besides the two of them there will be three other attendees: Andy (Ralph's trusted assistant) and two operations executives.

At the start of the meeting the following morning, Ralph's facial expression and terse tone of voice indicate that whatever had him in a cheerful mood the day before is long gone. The document Jenny prepared is handed to each participant. After a few minutes of reading time, Ralph throws his copy on the floor and shouts, "This is a piece of crap! Why is Andy the only person around here who knows how to write?"

After a few seconds of dead silence, during which no one moves a muscle, Jenny guesses from Ralph's facial expression that he realizes he has behaved badly. After another few seconds, he clears his throat, drops his volume, and says, "Well, let's move on." No one says a word about Ralph's outburst, and the rest of the meeting passes in a blur for Jenny. She feels relatively certain the others at the meeting are feeling awkward, too.

The next day Jenny gets a call from Andy, who asks if she has a moment to meet with him. She speculates he's calling about Ralph's misdemeanor at the meeting the previous day, and her interest in learning more about her boss and the company's inner political workings is heightened. When they get together, Andy opens their conversation by saying Ralph certainly had not meant to yell at her and goes on to say that Ralph is just so high-strung and intense that he sometimes becomes overly animated. Andy says he hopes that Jenny can get past the incident and adds that Ralph yells at him, too, but he's fine with it because Ralph is so brilliant.

Jenny knows that Ralph and Andy are both behaving like Clueless Emperors. Ralph's behavior in the meeting showed his cluelessness, and Andy's excuses for Ralph's poor behavior demonstrate how a Junior Clueless Emperor panders to the boss. Both use their power foolishly and selfishly. Ralph's behavior is like the emperor in Andersen's children's story who carries on with the parade even when he knows he's prancing around in his underwear, and Andy plays the role of the minister who pretends to see the cloth, when he cannot (see Appendix A). So how can Jenny best protect herself?

Strategy for Jenny: Jenny immediately accepts Andy's invitation (*Timing*). In their meeting, she does a lot of listening and not much talking in order to gather information (*Silence* and *Air Time*). Jenny is amazed by what she learns. Not only is Ralph capable of verbal abuse, but he uses a stand-in to make his apologies. She knows that her interaction with Andy has to be an award-winning performance which includes zero indication of any displeasure with Ralph (*Content*). At the same time, Jenny doesn't want to say anything she doesn't mean (*Content*). With a warm tone of voice, she says she appreciates Andy's call to talk about the incident (*Awareness*) and welcomes his candor (*Word Choice*). She makes no comment of any kind about Ralph's behavior (*Silence*).

Sure, she would prefer that Ralph apologize to her personally, but it's clear that's not going to happen. She could indulge herself and tell Andy she finds Ralph's behavior offensive, but that choice would be self-serving (*Awareness*). She knows Andy will report every meeting detail to Ralph, and anything she might reveal along those lines could hurt her. Ralph would be psychologically obligated to view her unfavorably to preserve his ego, and he might also find ways to punish her. Criticizing Ralph is clearly not an option (*Content*). Jenny responds with warmth (*Facial Expression,* and *Inflection*) and accepts the proxy apology, looking directly at Andy (*Eye Contact*), so he will perceive her as understanding and sincere.

Jenny knows her primary goal is to take care of herself, not to cure her Clueless Emperor Boss (*Content*). She builds rapport with Andy to ensure that Ralph—who will hear everything about this meeting later—has a neutral to positive impression of her. If his abusive behavior continues, Jenny may have to consider an exit strategy if she wants a civilized work environment. Because of Ralph's CEO status, she knows there isn't anyone with enough power to keep his potential for misconduct in check other than the board of directors, with whom Ralph is predictably well-behaved. Jenny isn't counting on him having an epiphany any time soon—she knows it's unlikely his personality is going to change (*Awareness*).

If she does nothing about the problem, she is colluding with a verbally abusive boss (as are her colleagues) and subtly condoning the mistreatment. Some companies have formal procedures and offer hotlines for internal complaints, but all too often Clueless Emperors run that show—don't assume senior management is trustworthy. It's important to thoroughly vet an organization's self-administered process before using it.

I know there are many people who submit to offensive behavior in their workplaces. With families to support, it's easy to rationalize being captive to circumstances. I sympathize, but making an unhealthy choice to stay in a nerve-racking environment is stressful. Taking steps to improve these situations shows much better sense. There are viable ways to move on. It's true that time, planning, and discipline are required, but doing nothing just delays the inevitable.

The first step is to learn the skills in this book. If the skills fail to take care of the problem because your Clueless Emperor is in the Bully category—or worse—and you don't have a support system of skilled, like-minded people, other means are required. When there is no indication that your Clueless Emperor will be departing any time soon, the next step is to do the research and find a reasonable workplace that respects people's dignity and spirit. Remaining in a state of denial is a slow but sure way to guarantee a demeaning environment that takes its toll on physical and mental health.

Clueless Emperor Case #8

Harry is a principal in a small architectural and design business, Customers-Come-First, Inc. It's a small firm and Harry likes it that way. He has a dozen employees who have been with him for years, and a client base that grows strictly through customer recommendations; no advertising necessary. Harry is proud of his accomplishments, passionate about his work, and fanatical about serving his clients. Most of Harry's customers do repeat business because he consistently provides a great product paired with great service.

One of Harry's long-term customers is a large city hospital system that generates significant revenue for his company. His contact there is Marian, with whom he has developed a good working relationship. She is a demanding, highly organized, and detail-oriented client, and Harry has consistently met or exceeded her expectations over the years. They have partnered on many large projects and work together so well that Marian once remarked they read each other's minds. Harry is confident their relationship is as solid as it gets.

A current project at the hospital involves outside suppliers who need information on routine matters that he and Marian have previously agreed to. He schedules a meeting with them at their location and doesn't copy Marian on the e-mail confirming the meeting. He does this partially out of neglect, but mostly because he's certain she would not want to attend. The day before the meeting, he's quite surprised to get a frosty e-mail from Marian questioning his lack of consideration in scheduling the appointment at the supplier's location—a one-hour commute for her each way—and berating him for being unprofessional by not letting her know about the meeting.

Marian has never used such words with him. He's surprised she even wants to attend. His error was one of omission rather than commission, so he hadn't given much thought to not advising her. Harry's commitment to customer service goes deep, and he's distraught about Marian's reaction to his slip. He can't concentrate on anything else out of concern for disappointing her. How can Harry patch things up with Marian?

Strategy for Harry: Pausing to think through Marian's complaint before shooting off a defensive e-mail (*Timing*), Harry recognizes that her anger is probably more related to being left out of the communication loop than because she wants to go to the meeting (*Content*). He knows any hint of a self-protective response on his part will exacerbate her frustration (*Awareness*). He also knows the need-to-be-right dynamic (*Emotion*) might be in play with Marian. Harry carefully reads and digests her message, then picks up the phone to call her (*Setting* and *Timing*).

Marian's anger hasn't dissipated, and she has a lot to say. Harry is quiet and listens without interrupting (*Silence* and *Air Time*). When she's finished, Harry takes full responsibility, uses a quiet tone of voice (*Volume*), and apologizes, saying he just wasn't thinking clearly when he forgot to include her on the message (*Word Choice*). He doesn't give an excuse of any kind, knowing that choice would be self-serving (*Awareness*). Any attempt to explain he hadn't thought she would want to attend isn't material to how she feels (*Content* and *Emotion*). Harry decides to use some light humor at the end of their conversation (*Content*) and asks Marian if he can have a hall pass (*Word Choice*) on this one, apologizes again, and offers to take her to lunch next week (*Setting*). Their history together coupled with Harry's non-defensive explanation should be enough to win Marian's forgiveness.

Clueless Emperor Case #9

Mary and Robert are a married couple with two young children. Both parents work outside the home—Mary significantly out-earns her husband. She takes advantage of this situation power by frequently implying that she provides more than half the family's income, so her husband needs to do more than half the work at home. She never says this directly, but communicates it in subtle, yet unmistakable ways.

Robert resents Mary's attitude at times. He was raised to believe the husband in a marriage should have position power by filling the role of primary breadwinner, and his dark side wishes his wife would pretend that's how their marriage works. At the same time, of course, he knows this is old-fashioned thinking, although he never forthrightly discusses this with her. He carries on as though they're a modern couple, but when there is an opportunity for him to seize power for himself and take it away from Mary, he jumps on it. And there are plenty of opportunities in any domestic partnership to do just that.

One Sunday evening Mary offers to plan the meal, grocery shop, and make dinner for the family the following evening. On Monday afternoon, however, an emergency work issue comes up that she feels must be addressed immediately, so this task becomes her priority. She leaves a phone message for Robert saying she'll be late, and doesn't mention her promise to make dinner. It's quite uncommon for Mary to break a commitment because of work problems, but it happens occasionally. She expects Robert will understand and acknowledge that she had no other realistic choice.

By the time she gets home that evening, the children have been fed and are sound asleep. Robert now feels he has a chit to play. He privately debates whether to use it right on the spot to let Mary know he's irritated, or should he simmer in silence instead? This is a common game that gets played in families every day. When people engage in passive aggressive behavior, and don't talk about frustrations or irritations as they arise, but dance around them instead, they create unnecessary tension and stress for themselves. It's the same situation in Andersen's fairy tale—the emperor would have been far better off acknowledging the reality of not seeing the cloth.

The conflict between Mary and Robert helps us see how situation power can easily shift back and forth between people who live together. This happens more often in family units than any other kind of relationship, because there aren't assigned hierarchical roles in families as there would be in a typical workplace. This lack of structured roles in families creates stress and lays the groundwork for controversy. When Mary canceled her dinner commitment, situation power went to Robert. In this case, both Mary and Robert have the choice to behave like Clueless Emperors or like Clued-In partners instead. Their relationship will grow stronger if they can let go of selfish motives and serve their common good. Great advice for all of us. What options do Mary and Robert have to prevent a conflict?

A Strategy for Mary: When Mary gets home that evening, the first thing she does (*Timing*) is apologize and let Robert know how appreciative she is that he understands why she had to stay late at work (*Timing*) and for feeding the children and getting them to bed. She ensures she doesn't over-talk (*Air*

Time) about her work situation or give unnecessary details of what caused her delay (*Awareness*). She asks Robert about his day (*Question*) and whether he has any preferences about what he would like for dinner (*Question*). She warmly suggests (*Volume, Eye Contact* and *Inflection*) they work together to make a delicious meal.

A Strategy for Robert: When Mary gets home that evening, Robert decides not to pounce on her for missing her commitment, because he knows the pressure she faces at work and doesn't want to add to it (*Content*). He has dinner ready for them to eat together (*Setting*). He asks her about the situation at work (*Question*) and doesn't interrupt her (*Timing*) while she's telling him all about it (*Awareness*). He looks at her as she's talking (*Eye Contact*) and nods his head (*Body Language*) as he discusses the work emergency with her (*Question*) to indicate his interest and show that he's listening.

> *"I practiced all the new skills relentlessly and now cannot be recognized from my old self."*
> —A Recovering Clueless Emperor

CHAPTER 17

When Success Is Not an Option

*"The effects of assholes are so devastating because they
sap people of their energy and esteem mostly through
the accumulated effects of small, demeaning acts, not so much
through one or two dramatic episodes."*
—Robert I. Sutton

During my career, I've coached hundreds of people whose problems and needs have given me the knowledge to develop a template of core skills that solve a wide variety of problems. These are the skills set forth in this book. It has been my experience that when people become consistently aware and behaviorally savvy, they can overcome most of the Clueless Emperors in their lives and become talented communicators at the same time.

If you're the target of a Clueless Emperor, or even an invested bystander, doing nothing is a useless choice—these problems don't fix themselves. Even though the next case takes place in a business setting, it's common for the same kind of oppression to exist in family units. It's especially heartbreaking when innocent children take the brunt of Clueless Emperors' aggressive behavior. Assisting those who cannot help themselves is best done with expertise—a good reason to learn the skills.

There will be occasions, however, when no skill in the world will relieve pressure. Clueless Emperors with very strong position power commonly surround themselves with flatterers who are afraid to speak up. This is how Clueless Emperors ensure there are no checks and balances to jeopardize their control. Their power allows them to do as they please, and the infrastructure they create makes it nearly impossible for victims to overcome them.

If you're in conflict with a very powerful Clueless Emperor, especially when facing the problem alone with no reinforcements, it's usually best to find expert, trustworthy assistance or look for a way out. Let's look at a final case where an exit is the most logical choice.

Clueless Emperor Case #10

Fred is the CEO and a major sharcholder of a privately-held manufacturing company, Know-It-All Inc. Fred has "inherited" this position from an uncle who recently retired, and shareholders and employees are skeptical that he has the ability to fill the role. The company has been successful over the years, demonstrated by overall financial growth and market share, but there have been a few financial downturns along the way when management decisions were not tactically or strategically sound. The company has withstood the test of time in the long term, and the past two years have been profitable. With all this success, Know-It-All has not yet snagged a Fortune 100 client, and Fred is eager to make that happen. He believes this will prove he's fit for his new role as CEO.

The firm is aggressive with its proposals to win the business of Fortune 100 clients, so within a year, Know-It-All is on a short list as a preferred vendor with seven potential new customers. This situation puts a lot of pressure on the business development department to assess how the company can simultaneously support this number of complex accounts if all the bids are successful. After a thorough analysis, they recommend that Know-It-All doesn't have the experience or resources to take on seven new accounts of this size. A formal presentation to the company's executives recommends that contracting with any more than two of these accounts isn't prudent, assuming current resources.

Fred doesn't like this recommendation. He pretends to be interested in perspectives other than his own, but his selfish focus doesn't fool anyone. He is determined to get his way and goes after all seven accounts by staging a campaign to gather support from other executives in the company. Slowly but surely, he wears down those who supported business development's recommendation to accept bids for no more than two of these new accounts. Over time, company executives who initially agreed to this approach become less vocal and discuss their disagreement with Fred only behind his back, because he's making their work environment uncomfortable. Unless they overtly agree with him, coming to work feels threatening. Unfortunately, Fred is successful in his quest, and Know-It-All is selected as the vendor by all seven companies.

We can all see where this is heading. Within two years, the balance sheet at Know-It-All is a river of red ink: shareholders vote to sell the company to avoid bankruptcy.

Strategy for Anyone Opposing Fred. This story represents a common Clueless Emperor challenge. The CEO of any company has a lot of position power, so Fred is going to be difficult, maybe impossible, for any one person in the organization to overcome, no matter how wrong Fred is. In this type of situation, risk assessment is imperative.

When people are caught in the web of a Clueless Emperor and his or her Apprentices, the chances of overcoming the Emperor are significantly diminished, unless the targets are skilled and band together. Left unchecked, Clueless Emperors eventually drive families into despair, organizations out of business, and countries into economic decline or war.

The skills in this book may not be enough to help a single individual save a family, likely not enough to save an organization, and certainly not enough to save a country from ruin, no matter how right and skillful that person may be. Some Clueless Emperors are just too powerful, and their intimidation factor can be considerable. That's why several skilled people banding together when very powerful Clueless Emperors are on the loose is such a good solution, but it's not always a viable option—there often aren't enough Clued-In people in the same place at the same time to form a coalition. It explains why so many families, organizations, and countries fail to survive.

I don't want to be pessimistic, but the advice here needs to be realistic. Disagreeing with powerful Clueless Emperors like Fred increases the risk of being ignored, ostracized, fired—or in extreme cases, exposed to physical harm. Developing skills and working together to overcome any highly powerful Emperor is what it takes to succeed. There really is strength in numbers if such a group could be organized.

When inappropriate or bad behavior exists in a family, organization, or country, remember that someone or some people with clout are allowing the oppressors to rule. People at the top levels of any hierarchy are role models of values and competence for the system they represent. Whenever incompetent people are left in charge, it's because those who could make a difference either turn a blind eye for self-serving reasons—or even actively support Clueless Emperors, sometimes out of fear. No organizational unit is immune. Several years ago the Catholic Church made headline news in this regard and more recently, Penn State. Clueless Emperors who commit criminal acts sometimes inhabit places where we least expect them.

This state of affairs is every bit as common in family units.

Structural and political hierarchies between organizations and families differ, but the fear factor can just as easily exist in both. Victimized family members often remain silent for this reason. Some of them eventually come forward, and by doing so, they remind us to be attentive to subtle calls for help when we hear them. And those who remain silent will never receive the support they are owed.

Just a few examples of well-known organizations crippled or destroyed by Clueless Emperors include Bethlehem Steel, Enron, AIG, Lehmann Brothers, Merrill Lynch, Digital Equipment, Borders, Blockbuster, and Kodak. Several airline companies also qualify—some of them repeatedly. I hope you will never have to contend with economic failures of this magnitude, or be in conflict with Clueless Emperors in the Bully or Beast categories. If you do, it's time to strongly consider moving on to saner surroundings when there isn't a realistic opportunity to overcome the problem.

The auto industry in Detroit came close to making this list, but with taxpayer dollars, the exit of several Clueless Emperors, and new Clued-In leaders taking their places, as of this writing, these American auto companies seem to be emerging from financial misery. It's a positive sign there are opportunities for improvement, even when the climate looks bleak. The city of Detroit itself has been brought to its knees by uncontrolled gangs of Clueless Emperors, some of them criminals. It went on for years, and we all watched as it happened. I love the city and hope it can regain its former glory with a critical mass of Clued-In citizens banding together.

Take responsibility for your own skill development and never blame other people or an environment as substitutes for your lack of competence. It's wiser to learn the skills, figure out the root causes of problems, and plan a reasonable strategy to succeed—even when that means an exit may be the best alternative. Get help if necessary. There is never a good excuse to sit idly by, giving tacit support, and hope that someone swoops in to save the day. Human nature being what it is, Clueless Emperors will continue to behave badly, sometimes get away with it, and cause failures. But here's the question we should ask: must there be so many?

I don't think so, and I hope you feel the same.

"Sometimes a Clueless Emperor just can't see the light in time and gets surprised when outside forces show up and take over. I never thought it would happen to me."
—A Toppled Clueless Emperor

CHAPTER 18

Final Thoughts

"Outliers are those who have been given opportunities—and who have had the strength and presence of mind to seize them."
—Malcolm Gladwell

I'd love to know your thoughts at this moment. Are you excited and ready to work on developing new skills? Or are you feeling anxious just thinking about the changes ahead? If so, it's understandable, but I promise the recommendations in this book are achievable and will help you overcome the Clueless Emperors in your future. Consistent discipline and practice, coupled with good-quality feedback, will yield a substantial payoff. It's not how you start this journey, but how you finish that counts. Lives have been transformed by taking on the challenge of gaining awareness and learning new physical skills that support good form. These skills bring power and peace of mind: struggles with Clueless Emperors are greatly reduced, if not all but eliminated. As a bonus, some Clueless Emperors who are overcome may even get Clued-In.

Awareness comes first. Without self-awareness, there isn't a way to calibrate the distance between current skill levels and your goals; nor will you be able to understand the emotions and non-verbal messages sent by others—it's difficult to interpret the entirety of any communication without this capacity. "Know thyself" is the starting point.

Remember to practice one skill at a time. Form a small dream team of trusted friends and/or colleagues who want to work together to learn the skills. I don't suggest, however, that you rely solely on one another for feedback. When everyone is in learning mode, it's all too easy to slip into giving positive feedback that's not yet earned. Skilled coaches will be needed from time to time to assess progress. Don't bypass this step—developmental feedback is invaluable.

I encourage daily practice using the skills. It's true that old habits die hard, but they can be killed. Disciplined practice creates new habits. As new behavioral skills become habits, your primary focus can return to the content of your communication. Once you have mastered the skills, it will be clear why the package wrapped around a message is such a critical factor for success. The learning is life-changing, and there isn't a better time to invest in your future than right now.

"Where there's a strong will, there's a way."
—A Recovering Clueless Emperor

Afterword

Dear Reader,

I wouldn't ask anyone to learn the skills in this book without relating my own experience in the land of Clueless Emperors. Although their bad behavior is common and has survived through the ages, I didn't personally notice them until I was a young adult. Of course, if it's true that Clueless Emperors are everywhere, as I now believe, they had to have been present in my environment; I just don't have any memories of them. Looking back, my lack of awareness could have been the innocence of youth, or perhaps the upshot of living in a small Midwestern city where polite behavior was the standard—it's a special and unique place—and I was fortunate to grow up there. Marc de Celle's book *How Fargo of You* (Third Edition, November 2011) is a great read and confirms my theory about the place where I was raised.

My undergraduate studies were completed close to home—I remained in the local area after graduation, teaching high school English in a small rural community nearby. As a result, my world remained insulated and certainly familiar, but it didn't stay that way for long. Two years later, life circumstances intervened and dictated a move to a larger city in another state. I quickly discovered that teaching positions were hard to come by in my new locale, so I had to get outside my comfort zone and consider other career options—it was a stressful time. Eventually a sales job in a large international company became available, and they were willing to take a chance on me. I was well aware that this position would be very different from anything I had ever experienced—but decided to take the risk.

The business world was a stunning departure from the small high school where I had worked, and provided an introduction to Clueless Emperor behavior. My new geography and workplace were like foreign countries, and my sense of vulnerability was at an all-time high. My heightened awareness was probably a result of being in unfamiliar surroundings—human beings usually pay closer attention to their environment when they're in the minority—not because Clueless Emperors don't exist in conservative Midwestern cities or educational institutions.

I was a trainee with no infrastructure who didn't know anything or anyone—and felt like an ant. Luckily, my education in Clueless Emperors 101 came through observation rather than firsthand experience. My own lack of power kept me off the radar screens of the Clueless Emperors in my workplace, which was a good thing at the time, because I certainly wasn't ready for them. I avoided conflict by sticking with the majority and generally keeping my thoughts to myself. Overcoming them was the last thing on my mind—I just wanted to avoid any encounters.

As time went by, I gained knowledge and skills through life experience and formal education and eventually drew some attention from Clueless Emperors. I was also becoming aware that my own behavior was part of the learning equation—the Clueless Emperor inside my brain took control from time to time. It became clear that I had to make choices about how to cope with the overall Clueless Emperor problem. My options as I saw them were to: 1) get run over and be a silent victim, 2) collude and stay out of firing range, 3) become a Junior Clueless

Emperor and study at the foot of the masters, or 4) learn the skills to overcome Clueless Emperor behavior and manage my own behavior to the best of my ability. Without much life experience at the time, I went down the path that seemed the most sensible. Years later, I'm glad the last option was my choice.

What I have painstakingly learned since making that decision so many years ago has provided the foundation for this book. Many skilled mentors and coaches have provided outstanding feedback, guidance, and role modeling to help me learn. Each new skill I discover becomes a building block for the next one—and my goal is to do my best to use them every day. When I slip, I get right back on the wagon, because I know the skills work.

The idea to write a book that would help people with their own Clueless Emperor problems first occurred to me semi-seriously in 2003, but that thought was daunting. I had always been a doer, not a writer—I used to avoid written tasks whenever possible—so I couldn't imagine taking on such a project. As an interim step, I got a notebook to keep track of concepts and skills that helped people overcome powerful, selfish oppressors. As life presented new problems, the techniques that solved them were added to the notebook—but any kind of "real book" was still a long way off in my mind. As the years went by, and the notebooks multiplied, the idea to write something in a formal, organized way became more compelling.

Fast forward to August, 2009: I won't forget the day when I sat down to write with a vision of a book actually swirling around in my brain. I felt naively ready. The words poured out, and a 25,000-word draft took just six weeks to finish. I felt so proud—until the first feedback I received was that my little book was more painful to read than getting a root canal. Word choice aside, I knew it was true. I thought about quitting—I sort of wanted to quit. But Clueless Emperors cause so much unnecessary grief that I felt duty-bound to share what I had learned over a decades-long career. Helping people find ways to overcome Clueless Emperors became my mission, but the question of how to convert my knowledge into words loomed large.

So my first attempt failed—so what? I thought. Following one's own advice need not be such a formidable task! In the spirit of this book, I had to learn to convey the content in my head to the outside world in good written form—but clearly, this was going to be a challenge.

With the "what" in my head, I labored over "how" to get the message across in an understandable way. Four years and (what seems like) a million additions, rewrites, and edits later, I'm satisfied the book's readability beats getting a root canal. If your Clueless Emperor education is less bumpy than it otherwise might have been without the information you've gained here, the mission I set out to achieve will have been realized. Thank you very much for reading—put your new skills to good use.

Warm regards,
Victoria

Appendix A

Hans Christian Andersen's
"The Emperor's New Clothes"

For those who may have missed this children's tale or perhaps no longer recall the details, here is my retelling of the story.

Long ago, in a kingdom far away, lived an emperor whose reason for living was a devotion to accumulating the finer things in life. He was always on the lookout for how to best pamper himself. His kingdom and subjects were of no importance to him other than to serve his needs, and over time, everyone in the surrounding region knew about the emperor's foolish and selfish ways.

Of all the luxuries the emperor coveted, beautiful clothes were at the top of his list. The emperor spared no expense when it came to his wardrobe. One day, as it happened, two swindlers were passing through the area and heard about this foolish, selfish emperor and his love of clothes. As they were short on cash at that particular time, they decided to take advantage of an opportunity to shore up their financial position.

Posing as high-end weavers and fashion consultants, the tricksters gained easy entrance into the palace and made a sales pitch to the emperor that he found enticing: they had, they said, the materials and craftsmanship to weave the most sumptuous fabric ever made. They further promised to sew stunning royal robes using the opulent material if the emperor found the cloth to be exquisite. The price tag for all this would be quite high, they admitted, but the benefits would far exceed the expense. Then in quiet voices that upped the emperor's interest, the weavers suggested the fabric would have the magical quality of being invisible to fools and to those unfit for their jobs.

The emperor was captivated. He had never heard of such unusual material. He considered that, although costly, the royal robes would provide an added benefit beyond the sheer beauty of the fabric: the emperor could use his new clothes to evaluate the worthiness of his employees. Unable to resist, he didn't have to ponder very long. *Well worth the expense*, he reasoned as he wrapped up his cost-justification concerns and gave the order to proceed forthwith.

The characteristics of the cloth's unique qualities soon leaked outside the palace walls and created quite a buzz, becoming the talk of the town. The emperor was flattered by the curiosity of the townspeople and was thrilled that the beautiful clothes would soon belong to him alone. At the same time, however, he was a bit nervous about the cloth being invisible to fools and people unfit for their jobs. A bit of self-doubt even crept into his mind. *Will I be able to see it?* he asked himself. *Of course, I will. There isn't a reason to think otherwise—but what if I cannot?*

To be on the safe side, while the cloth was being loomed, the emperor decided to send his wisest and most trusted minister to check out the weavers' progress. *If this loyal, competent friend can see it*, the emperor said to himself, *then I'll be completely confident about the merits of the cloth.* So began the emperor's problems.

At the royal request, his favorite minister visited the weavers to inspect their work. Upon entering the chamber, he was astonished to see them toiling over empty looms. A major wave of alarm spread through him—he could not see the cloth. Of course, in reality they were "weaving" nothing but air, but the minister hadn't considered that possibility. He had fully expected to see the cloth. Without question, he didn't think himself a fool; nor did he consider himself unfit for his job. But he felt pressured to protect himself and anxiously wondered what to do. As the seconds ticked by, he knew he had to think fast.

As the swindlers pretended to unfurl the magnificent cloth, this wise minister did not have the self-assurance to declare, "Hey, wait a minute—I don't see anything! What's going on here?" He so desperately craved the emperor's approval. Without the self-confidence that appropriate skills would have given him, he was scared silent. In fear of losing his job, he unwisely chose the path of collusion. He subtly prodded the swindlers for a description of the fabric, memorized what they said, and made a hasty exit.

With his head hanging in misery, he returned to the palace. As the deflated minister entered the throne room, he found the emperor waiting breathlessly. This "wise" minister then unwisely chose to tell a lie to assure his place in the empire. He quietly reported the elaborate beauty of the cloth as told to him by the swindlers. As the emperor "listened" to his minister, his self-absorbed state caused him not to notice the trembling voice he heard, or see the pain in his friend's eyes. Quite the contrary. He was selfishly pleased beyond words and could hardly wait to possess the cloth for himself.

In great anticipation, therefore, the emperor immediately ordered the weavers to bring the cloth to the palace and asked his favorite and most trusted minister to join him. When the weavers arrived and unrolled the pretend-cloth, imagine his horror. A wave of panic rolled over him—he couldn't see it. He blinked a few times and mentally scrambled to collect his thoughts. The weavers began smiling and nodding in delight over the scene, which the emperor interpreted as their sense of pride in weaving the fabric. In reality, of course, they were rejoicing over the early signs of a successful scam. In silence, and knowing full well there was little time to make his next move, the anxious emperor leaned down close and pretended to scrutinize the weavers' workmanship.

He couldn't believe his bad luck—the greatest emperor of all time! What was going on? Growing ever more frantic by the moment, the emperor hesitated. *Was it possible he was a fool, unfit for his job? No, it can't be true—I just need to stall for time.* With as much false confidence as he could muster, he raised himself up to full height and decreed another viewing was in order: his best and brightest courtiers were commanded to the throne room to have a look.

Of course, they too pretended to see the cloth and feigned admiration and envy, sighing over its splendor. Unfortunately, their performance was convincing. Now certain the cloth was real, the distressed and depressed emperor spoke. Ever the consummate actor, he lavished praise on its beauty and instructed the weavers to stitch together the royal robes. Keeping up a good front, he announced there would be a procession through town on the date the weavers were scheduled to deliver the new threads to the palace. What kind of emperor would he be if he didn't want to show off this exquisite new addition to his wardrobe?

On the big day, the weavers arrived at the palace and grandly presented the emperor's new clothes. Now psychologically prepared for pretense, the emperor staged an outstanding pantomime as he pretended to try them on. His top staff was in attendance, and they "oohed" and "aahed" at how magnificent the emperor looked. Meanwhile, outside the palace, the pressure was on. The townspeople were lined up, waiting for the procession to begin. When the emperor was "dressed," he twirled around and strutted down the stairs of the palace to begin the parade. As he began his march up the promenade, his stunned subjects gaped, not knowing how to react to their emperor wearing only his underwear. It took a few seconds, but they collectively summoned up a politically correct response and cried out with various renditions of "Oh, emperor, how regal and handsome you are!"

But just then, amid all the hubbub, a child in the crowd looked up at his father in total bewilderment. "But he has nothing at all on," whispered the confused boy.

The child's father, understanding crowd dynamics full well, paused and decided to risk repeating his son's words in a louder tone so others nearby could hear. "My son here says the emperor has nothing at all on," he said with a chuckle, just in case no one else would be courageous enough to acknowledge the obvious. Everyone could see quite well the emperor was wearing only his underwear, so bolstered by the father's comment, they repeated his words.

Like juicy gossip, the headline rippled through the crowd—thank goodness for strength in numbers. The obvious reality was soon fully exposed. Of course, by the time it reached the emperor's ears, he finally realized the reality of his situation: the "weavers" had conned him. And with this understanding came the awareness he had been prancing half naked down the promenade. As he stood there considering all available options, looking like the fool he was, he made a classic Clueless Emperor choice. To the utter astonishment of his subjects, he squared his shoulders, smiled as though nothing was wrong, and gave the order to continue the festivities. He continued the march through town in his underwear with his knights and ministers trailing behind him, carrying the train of a robe that everyone knew did not exist.

Appendix B

Answers to Quiz in Chapter 7

BEHAVIORS? ... OR PERCEPTIONS?

- Hard Worker (P)
- Smile (B)
- Cooperative (P)
- Read the report (B)
- Creative (P)
- Pleasant (P)
- Adequate (P)
- Arrived early (B)
- Won the game (B)
- Abrupt (P)
- Wrote a note (B)
- Supportive (P)
- Expert (P)
- Listened (P)

- Traveled to Texas (B)
- Sent an e-mail (B)
- Bought groceries (B)
- Poor performer (P)
- Made a sandwich (B)
- Participative (P)
- Eye contact (B)
- Arrived late (B)
- Walked the dog (B)
- Friendly (P)
- Dominating (P)
- Top performer (P)
- Shrugged (B)
- Enthusiastic (P)

- Nice person (P)
- Responsible (P)
- Attended class (B)
- Certain (P)
- Absent (B)
- Silent (B)
- Quiet (P)
- Sat down (B)
- Effective (P)
- Waved (B)
- Spoke out (P)
- Treated fairly (P)
- Said "no" (B)
- Trustworthy (P)

ACKNOWLEDGEMENTS

This book was a four-year project with fits and starts along the way—from a high-energy focus to a let's-take-some-time-off-I-can't-do-this attitude on my part. I look back and know that because a wide variety of family, friends, and colleagues contributed creative ideas, thoughtful feedback, encouragement, and editing assistance, I was able to make this book happen. In no particular order I am grateful to:

Kim Sharkey, Maria Chasins, Melinda Sumurdy, Kevin Kelly, Elaine Sage, Sophie de Caen, Sam Rittenberg, Susan Smith, Carl Kleeman, Corinne Casper, Shellie Unger, Marc Levy, Jeanne Murphy, Krista Sprenger, Alan Pickman, Cheryl Greenhalgh, Donna Garcia, Kathy Facione, Tom Tanner, Connie Katsaros, Leif Billings, Jeanine Knudson, Allen McNeill, Jane McNeill, Kathleen Mullens, Craig Hurst, Susan LaVallee, Linda Swenson Baker, Kamal Chachra, Nancy Dreicer, Lynne Schultz and Jon Phillips.

Many thanks to those who gave their valuable time to read, discuss, and critique.

Barbara Ardinger, my editor, and Nancy Cleary, my publisher, were indispensable.

My parents, Tom and Joan Humphrey, edited and encouraged. Their contributions cannot be over-emphasized.

My brother, Buzz Humphrey, was my rock.

INDEX

30714410R00178

Made in the USA
Lexington, KY
13 March 2014